A Textbook

OF

Linguistics & Phonetics

Linguistics & Phonetics

A Textbook
OF
Linguistics & Phonetics

Dr. Jaydeep Sarangi

KOLKATA

Published by
Books Way
Publishers & Distributors
86A College Street (Y.M.C.A. Building)
Kolkata - 700 073
Ph.: 91-33-2257 2423 / 2257 2476
E-mail: bookswaypub@rediffmail.com
Visit us: www.booksway.in

© Publisher

ISBN: 81-89293-07-9

All rights reserved. No part of this publication may be reproduced, copied or transmitted, in any form or by any means, without permission of the copyright holder.

First Published: 2006
Second Revised Edition: 2008
Third Revised Edition: 2009
Fourth Revised Edition: 2011

Price: Rupees One Hundred Fifty Only

Printed by
STARLINE
19/H/H, Goa Bagan Street
Kolkata - 700 006

Letter Setting
BHOLANATH CHATTERJEE
59, Ramgarh Colony, Narasingh Avenue
Dum Dum, Kolkata-700 074
Contact: 9831307687

In Memory
of
Niranjan Mohanty
(1953-2008)

"Every day
I check the mirror
to be sure
if the reflection is
mine."

From 'Self', Stephen Gill

Acknowledgements

This revised edition of my text evolved from my continuing collaboration in teaching Modern Grammar at Vidyasagar University, W.B. Classroom experience, as well as engaging feedback from my academic friends, students and colleagues, revealed ways in which materials from the previous edition could be improved.

Despite changes I have incorporated certain aspects of the book which remain unchanged. My focus is on the basic conceptual foundation of modern grammar. I've tried to relate it to literary texts.

Assuming that the majority of the readers are the second language speakers of English, I have drawn linguistic data exclusively from English. Today, English in India is seen as just another Indian language. I take up some specific examples.

I shall be happy if this edition comes to help the students/ research scholars for whom it is written.

I have tried to make the learning of Language / Linguistics & Phonetics enjoyable and as human as possible. For the evolution of this third editon I would like to thank my academic friends in India and abroad.

I owe more than I can say to numerous predecessors in the field of *Linguistics and Phonetics*. However, as the title implies, it is a *Textbook-cum-Guide*. An important feature of this edition is its carefully annotated bibliography and index.

I thank the publisher for publishing the book elegantly.

Dr. Jaydeep Sarangi

PREFACE TO THE FIRST EDITION

Linguistics and *Phonetics* are comparatively new disciplines. This book has been written for the students of Linguistics and Phonetics of Indian Universities. I make no claim for originality. The ideas expressed and the principles explained are those of renowned scholars and researchers in the respected disciplines. To illustrate several points, I have consulted standard available books and journals on the subjects whenever necessary.

I acknowledge my indebtedness to my teachers of Linguistics, Phonetics, English Language Teaching (ELT) and English Literature with sincerity and gratitude. I also express my gratitude and indebtedness to the authority and staff of Seva-Bharati Mahavidyalaya, Kapgari, Midnapure, West Bengal for inspiring me at the formative period of the book. I offer my sincere thanks to my colleagues and friends. I express my regards to my relatives, family friends and my parents who constantly goaded me to write this book. I was very fortunate in having 'a friend' who helped me in the process of 'proof correction'. I offer my sincere thanks to Sk. Salauddin of Books Way who has helped me by publishing this book.

Constructive comments on the book and suggestions for its improvement are expected from knowledgeable quarters. I shall be happy if the book comes to help the students for whom it is written.

Jhargram   **Dr. Jaydeep Sarangi**
18.07.2003

PREFACE TO THE BOOKS WAY EDITION

This first revised edition has involved updating throughout the book including an updating of all the references. The book focuses on basic concepts in Linguistics and Phonetics Covering the syllabus of most Indian Universities which offer linguistics and phonetics as a subject in Hons. and M.A. (English) course. The book is divided into two parts. *Part I* deals with linguistics and its applied aspects, and *Part II* deals essentially with Phonetics, and an Index has been added to help the inquisitive learners. Many sections extensively revised include those dealing with instructions to both Indian and Foreign students and with acoustic information (for which new spectograms have been produced). To illustrate several points, illustrations have been drawn from English and some Indian languages.

Basically this edition, *inter alia*, focuses on some very contemporary and relative new issues related to ELT (English Language Teaching). However, for evolution of this revised edition. I am grateful to Alice Spencer (Italy), Lety Alterno (UK), A. Arunachalam & Yemen), G.S. Jha (Tezu) and Priya Hosali (Hyderabad). I am also grateful to Dr. Stephen Gill (Canada) and Dr. Bibhu Padhi for their beautiful poems.

My thanks also go to SK. Salauddin and Mr. Asutosh Roy, Journalist— Editio for removing errors in the revised edition.

Jhargram   Dr. Jaydeep Sarangi
July, 2005

PREFACE TO THE SECOND EDITION

This edition of the book is an attempt to offer a precise and analytical study of English *Linguistics* and *Phonetics*. The edition treats exhaustively, with copious illustrations, the theories of Linguistics and Applied Linguistics. The parameters of Linguistics and Phonetics are thoroughly discussed and different forms are explained with the help of available illustrations.

The book serves the needs of students studying at different Universities as well as the budding scholars and teachers of the concerned field. Postcolonial Linguistic Space is a subject of debate in any social and literary discourse dealing with theoretical grounding related to place and displacement. The twin process of subversion of the cultural milieu and the re-placing of Queen's Tongue has been elaborately discussed in the chapter: *Application of Linguistics*. This edition of the book sets out to open the possible limits of the Postcolonialism as a literary/social discourse. I have tried to explore the subject referring to different genres in connection with their traditional and radical interpretation into consideration.

The edition could not have been in the hands of the readers without the most useful comments and timely suggestions received from knowledgeable quarters. I thank Professor Isabel Gonzalez-Cruz, Professor Dora Sales, Professor Alejandra Moreno Alvarez and Professor D. Parameswari for their generous suggestions. This book is the fruit of my interaction with the Fellows and Associate Fellows at the Indian Institute of Advanced Study, Shimla (H.P.) during my first spell of UGC-Associateship. I must acknowledge with gratitude of Professor Umesh Bagade, Professor Kailash Pattanaik, Dr. Archana Verma, Dr. Nirmal Kumar and Dr. Ajanta Sircar for their valuable suggestions and meaningful verbal discourse with me. I shall be failing in my sense of duty if I do not mention the support I received from my parents, wife and daughters. My family members are my strength. They don't imprison me in mundane stereotype family matters unnecessarily.

I thank the publisher for taking utmost care of my book and publishing this edition within a minimum length of time.

Jhargram Dr. Jaydeep Sarangi
October, 2007

CONTENTS

PART I: LINGUISTICS & APPLIED LINGUISTICS

Language and Linguistics	1
Word Classes	4
Morphology	8
IC Analysis	18
Phrases & Clauses	23
Structural Linguistics and Phonology	52
Deep Structure & Ambiguity of Sentences	58
Article Features	80
Phrase Structure Rules	83
Social Aspects of Language	90
Main Branches of Linguistics	94
Application of Linguistics in Literary Discourse	99
Language in Education Policy Since Independence	109
Methods of Teaching English	113
Two Great Orissan Pilgrims : A Sociolinguistic Study	134
Bibliography	138

PART II: PHONETICS

Phonetics & Organs of Speech	141
Classification of Sounds	148
Description of Consonants, Vowels & Diphthongs	153
Phonetic Transcription	160
Structure of the Syllable and Phoneme Sequence	162
Word Accent	165
Accent, Rhythm and Intonation	168
Spoken English in India	174
Bibliography	177
Index	178

CONTENTS

PART I: LINGUISTICS & APPLIED LINGUISTICS

Language and Linguistics	1
Word Classes	4
Morphology	8
IC Analysis	18
Phrases & Clauses	23
Structural Linguistics and Phonology	42
Deep Structure & Ambiguity of Sentences	48
Article/Feature	50
Phrase Structure Rules	58
Social Aspects of Language	69
Main Branches of Linguistics	80
Application of Linguistics in Literary Discourse	89
Language in Education Policy Speech Indoctrination	100
Methods of Teaching English	115
Two Great Orators Pilgrims: A Sociolinguistic Study	125
Biblio-maps	136

PART II: PHONETICS

Phonetics & Organs of Speech	141
Classification of Sounds	148
Description of Consonants	
Vowel & Diphthongs	153
Phonetic Transcription	160
Structure of the Syllable and Phoneme Sequence	162
Word Accent	165
Accent, Rhythm and Intonation	168
Spoken English in India	174
Bibliography	177
Index	178

LANGUAGE AND LINGUISTICS

Introduction

Communication is a basic human activity. In the animal world, communication is based on a set of signals; man, on the contrary, has a sophisticated system of communication, human language. Language is a mirror of mind in a deep significant sense. It is a "product of human intelligence, created anew in each individual by operations that lie far beyond the reach of will or consciousness." (Chomsky, 1975 : 3–4)

It is a symbol system based on arbitrary convention. Language has a great structural complexion. Human language is infinitely extendable and modifiable according to the changing needs and conditions of the users. Noam Chomsky in his book *Language and Mind* (1972) claims language as "unique to man", which constitutes the "human essence". Creativity or resourcefulness is the hallmark of human language. The biological side of the language is the subject of increasing research. Whenever any disease or injury affects the left side of the brain, some aspect of the ability to perceive, process, or produce language may be disturbed. Individuals in such a brain disease are said to be aphasir, and their language disorder gives us insight into how the human brain carries out its language-related tasks. Where is language localized in the brain? The answer is obviously the posterior inferior part of the frontal lobe in the left cerebral hemisphere, now known as Broca's area (the motor speech area; *see figure 1*)

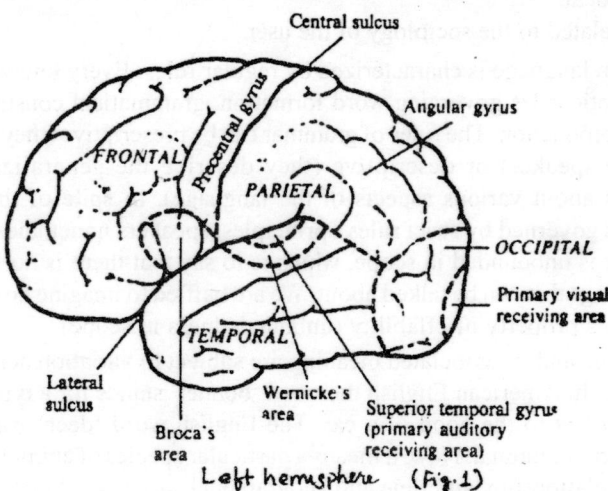

Left hemisphere (Fig. 1)

Today neuro-psychologists agree that specific neuroanatomic structures, generally of the left hemisphere, are vital for speech and language production.

Birds have their wings. Similarly, man has language. The wings give birds its peculiar attitude for aerial locomotion. Language enables man's intelligence. It is a mode of self-representation. The learners come to the task of language learning with a sophisticated device which enables him to learn language with a little more assistance from the teacher than the provision of comprehensible input. Language is the expression of ideas by means of speech signals combined into words (meaningful). Language never ceases to change; it is always in a state of flux. It is not just a logical system of structural dependence; it is also a social phenomenon. The Context of Situation is a deciding factor of language in use. The nature of participants (in discourse), topic of discourse, role of the participants, socio-pragmatic context, the function of speech events—language is a combination of all these factors. The ability to use language appropriately (in appropriate context) is one's communicative competence.

Some Features of Language

(i) It is symbolic.
(ii) Language is human activity.
(iii) It is open-ended.
(iv) Language is modifiable and extendable.
(v) It is logical / systematic.
(vi) It is arbitrary by nature.
(vii) It is a mode of self-expression.
(viii) It is vocal.
(ix) It is related to the sociology of the user.

Human language is characterized by regular rules. Every known language has systematic rules governing word formation, grammatical construction and pragmatic production. The rules of grammar can be prescriptive (they prescribe / dictate the speaker) or descriptive (they describe the generalizations and regularities about various aspects of the language). In spite of the fact that language is governed by strict rules / principles, speakers nonetheless control a system that is unbounded in scope, which is to say that there is no limit to the kinds of things that can be talked about. We are baffled to imagine how language achieves this property of effability (unboundedness in scope).

Language and its associated meaning are subject to variation across groups of speakers. In American English the word 'bonnet' stands for a type of hat, in Britain it refers to the hood of a car. The English word 'deer' was once the general word for animal. Now, it means a particular species of animal. Historical change in relationship with time and geographical space is not rare.

What is Linguistics? Fundamentally, the field is concerned with the nature of language and communication. Linguists try to formulate descriptive rules on language. The important assumption that linguists make is that the various human languages constitute a unified phenomenon. The job of a linguist is to construct theory analysing linguistic data and to predict the potential date.

Inadequacies of Traditional Grammar

Structuralists put emphasis on structure of linguistic analysis. They discovered several deficiencies / inadequacies in the traditional grammar. They termed these inadequancies as 'Fallacy': Latinate Fallacy, Semantic Fallacy, Logical Fallacy, Historical Fallacy, Written Form Fallacy, etc.

Linguistics and Sanskrit Grammar

Contemporary Linguistics has branched off into several scientific disciplines many of which are inter-disciplinary. Some branches of linguistics have taken up seminal ideas from Pānini. A few of the linguists have themselves admitted to having derived inspiration from analogues to Pānini. Ferdinand de Saussure was a Professor of Sanskrit. His theories have affinities with Bhartrihari's *Prakritadhvani* and *Vaikritadhvani*. According to Leonard Bloomfield (1953 : 11), Pānini's concept of 'lopa' (zero) has been "in practice eminently serviceable device " of linguistic explanation of irregular forms. The forms such as singular 'sheep' and plural 'sheep', deer (sing), and deer (pl.), etc.; past and past participle forms like 'cut'—'cut'—'cut', are explained as zero-alterants. Bloomfield and his followers use it with reference to Phonology, Morphology and even Syntax. An infinitive without 'to' is termed as zero-infinitive. As the level of word formation Pānini has a significant influence on the linguist. The processes of '*Sandhi*' forms have been used and applied in English. George Cardona in *Pānini* : *A Survey of Research* (1980) gives an authentic opinion of several linguists who find in Pānini striking parallels to linguistic insights present in the *Astādhyāyi*. Pānini researchers find similarities between Pāninian *Karaka* theory and Fillmore's case grammar. Firthian school of linguists has been greatly influenced by Pānini. David Crystal in his book, *Linguistics* (1980 : 45) claims that Pāninian principles are "still used in modern linguistics".

The Tenets of Modern Linguistics

(i) All languages in the world are potentially equal.
(ii) There is nothing called 'corrupt' or 'pure' language.
(iii) Spoken language is primary.
(iv) Linguistic Changes are natural to all languages.
(v) Linguistics is a descriptive science.
(vi) Language decline is a natural process.

WORD CLASSES

Traditional grammarians have often defined parts of speech in terms of their meaning and function. For example, a noun is defined as the name of a place, person or thing and an adjective is defined as a word which qualifies a noun as in "a ceiling fan".

There are some grammarians who place words in certain definite categories or classes. These classes are : nouns, verbs, adjectives, pronouns, adverbs, wh-words, demonstratives and particles, etc.

Nouns—Nouns control actions (as subjects).

Actions can be directed to them too (as objects / complements).

Nouns can be identified easily:
(i) It takes plural inflections:
   cat + s = cats.
   box + es = boxes.
(ii) It is used after 'determiners':
   'a book'
   Here 'a' is a determiner.
(iii) It can take possessive inflection:
   (a) Ram's.
   (b) Robot's
(iv) Usually, it is used before the verb:
   (a) The **sky** is clear today.
   (b) **University** is the place for higher education.

Pronouns (Personal)—It takes the place of nouns or nominal groups. It can be both 'subject-type' and 'object-type' :

Subject-type :   I—We,
                 He—She
Object-type :   Me—Us,
                 Him—Her (also subj.-type)

Examples in sentences :
   She studies at Kalyani University. (subj.)
   I want to meet **her**. (obj.)

Verbs—Verbs are the action /doing words. Verbs can take different forms in a sentence:
(i) 'infinite' form (to go)
(ii) 'bare infinitive' form (go)
(iii) '-s' form (goes)
(iv) 'past' form (went)
(v) 'progressive' form (going)

Verbs can be transitive and intransitive.

Word Classes

Adjective—It indicates the quality, conditions and the status of nouns. It can be used in two ways :
(i) attributive use (preceding the noun)
(ii) predicative use (following the noun)

Adverbs—Adverbs qualify the verbs, adjectives and other adverbs. It generally follows verbs. Certain adverbs like 'never', 'often' etc., precede the verbs. Most of the adverbs have '-*ly*' as suffix.

Adverbs can be of different types :
(i) ending in '-ly' (Example—cordially)
(ii) not ending in '-ly' (Example—low, high etc.)
(iii) with certain prefixes (Example—ahead)
(iv) with some suffixes (Example—towards)

Wh-words—These words are used for asking questions (Interrogative sentences). These words are also used to make relative links :
The man who wrote *The Guide* is dead.

Demonstratives—It indicates person / thing referred to. For example, this, that, these, etc.

Particles—It indicates the direction, the connection and some other relevant things. Particles can be of different kinds:
binding particles—if, since etc.
linking particles—and, or, but etc. (conjunctions)
adverbial particles—the play is *over* etc.
intensifying particles—too, very etc.
verbs particles—set *in*, set *out* etc.

We have some other classes of words too. These classes are discussed below :

Ordinal—It defines thing's position in a series:
third, second, twentieth, etc.

Cardinal—Cardinals are the numbers:
two, three, twenty, etc.

Quantifier—Which express quantity.
Example : all, some, etc.

Determiner—It includes articles, possessive nouns, pronouns and demonstratives.

There can be pre-determiner (pre-det.) too:
All these boys from a Govt. School.

Here 'all' is pre-det, 'these' is demonstrative (which comes under the umbrella of det.)

'det' stands for derterminer.

Classifier—When Nouns act as adjectives, are known as classifiers: All the Boys from a **Govt.** school.

In this sentence 'Govt.' is noun but acts as an adjective. Therefore, the class of 'Govt.' is classifier.

Now we shall level the words in the following sentences in respect of their classes :

(i) The   tall   boy   put   those   toys   on   the   ground.
        det.   adj.   n.   vb.   det.   n   prep.   det.   n.
        (article)   (demonstrative)   (article)

(ii) I   believe   that   Niren   knows   the   fact.
        pron.   vb.   conj.   n.   vb.   det.   n.
                                                  (article)

(iii) The   room   looked   good.
         det.   n.   vb.   adj.
         (article)

(iv) Anil   meets   the   tragic   destiny.
         n.   vb.   det.   adj.   n.
                         (art.)

(v) He   is   a   member   of   the   Association
       pro.   vb.   det.   a.   prep.   det.   n.
       n.   (art.)   (art.)

Nouns: Gender

A noun that denotes a male is to be of the **Masculine Gender**.

Nouns like Mr. Nayar, George Mathew, Pritam, son are said to be of masculine gender.

A noun that denotes a female is to be of the **Feminine Gender**.

Nouns like Mrs. Nayar, Dora Sales, Rita, daughter are said to be of feminine gender.

A noun that denotes a lifeless thing is said to be of the **Neuter Gender**: Computer, moboile phone, blackboard, book, etc.

Pronouns and Person:

Dr. Mahapatra is a Professor of Physics. He belongs to Cuttack. He is a poet. Mrs. Dutta is a housewife. She lives at Puri. She likes to read contemporary novels in English.

Words like 'he' and 'she' are called pronouns. Pronouns stand for 'for a noun'. There are seven pronouns in English: I, we, you, he, she, it, they.

The noun for which a pronoun stands is its antecedent.

Personal pronouns stand for three persons:
(a) The person speaking—First Person
(b) The person speaking to—Second Person
(c) The person spoken of—Third Person

EXERCISES

Label the word-classes of the following sentences. (One has been done for you) :

1. "Tom Jones" is a picaresque novel.

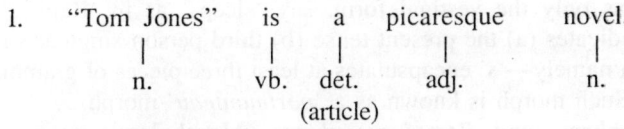

    n.   vb.   det.   adj.   n.
                (article)

2. I met the students from Kerala.
3. Life is a sad tale.
4. Conrad wrote many famous novels.
5. Gunesekara is a Srilankan novelist.
6. He read Nahal's 'Azadi'.
7. Kaberi wrote a letter to her best friend in Pune.
8. Tom Jones is an unheroic hero.
9. Defoe began his career in journalism.
10. This novel is not merely an adventure story.
11. Joyce left Dublin in 1904 for Paris.
12. 'Life' is the best word in the Dictionary.
13. A wolf and a fox conspired to kill a lot of other animals.
14. 'ELT' should be in the University syllabus.
15. I have great regards for Mr. Hota.
16. Tactile, Visual and Aural are three principal modes of communication.
17. 'Notions' are concepts that language can express.
18. Jin Young remains Hong Kong's best-known writer.
19. Hayim Hazaa voiced his disgust for contemporary Israeli writing.
20. Pasolini was not just a novelist.

MORPHOLOGY

Morphology deals with word as the basic unit, how affixes are attached to stems. A morpheme is a minimal meaningful unit. A morpheme is essentially an abstract construct. For example, the *past tense morpheme* in English; which is realised in various ways in the examples below :
want—wanted, run—ran, give—gave, feel-felt, cut—cut.
Morphology is the study of morphemes. *Morph* means shape. In 'wash—washed' pair the past tense *morpheme* is realised as—*ed*. That is, -*ed* is the morph. The various realisations of a morpheme are called its allomorph. A morph may not have overt realisation, as in sheep—sheep pair and cut—cut pair. These are the examples of zero morph.

sheep +	$\phi \rightarrow$	sheep
(Male)	zeromorph	(Female)
cut +	$\phi \rightarrow$	cut
(Present)	zeromorph	(Past)

English has only the vestigal form, say 'sleeps' as in 'Rajib sleeps' where—'s' indicates (a) the present tense (b) third person singular subject. So one morph namely—'s' encapsulates at least three pieces of grammatical information. Such morph is known as a *'portmanteau'* morph.

Free morpheme and *Bound morpheme*—Morphology assumes that words have internal structure. For example, 'unnecessarily'.

'Unnecessarily' can be morphologically cut into three pieces. *Un*—, necessary, -*ly*, 'Necessary' can stand by itself whereas *un*- and -*ly* cannot exist independently. 'Necessary' is an example of free morpheme (which has the freedom to stand independently) and *un*- and -*ly* are bound morphemes (they cannot exist independently).

Similarly, in 'unhappiness' *un*- and -*ness* are bound morphemes and 'happy' is a free morpheme.

Stem, Root and Affix—In 'unnecessarily' the two bound morphemes are attached to 'necessary' which is the stem. 'Root' is the ultimate (which cannot be divided further) of any free morpheme. In this example 'necessary' is both 'stem' and 'root'. 'Stem' can be divided (morphologically) further.

In the above example, *un*- and -*ly* are affixes when *un*- is a prefix (which is attached before the 'stem') and -*ly* is a suffix (which is attached after the 'stem'). Apart from prefix and suffix, there are the elements which are sometimes added in the middle of the stem, they are called *infix*. English has no infixes. Tagolog has plenty of such infixes. For example,

'Sulat' means 'write'.
Sumulat means 'make write'.

Here—*mu*—is the infix. Prefix, Suffix and Infix together is called *Affix*. Free morphemes allow bound morphemes to be appended to them. Most of the forms have a tendency to extend by allowing bound forms to be stuck to them. This process is known as 'affixation'. It is really an important aspect of language. It is crucial and important to Morphology too.

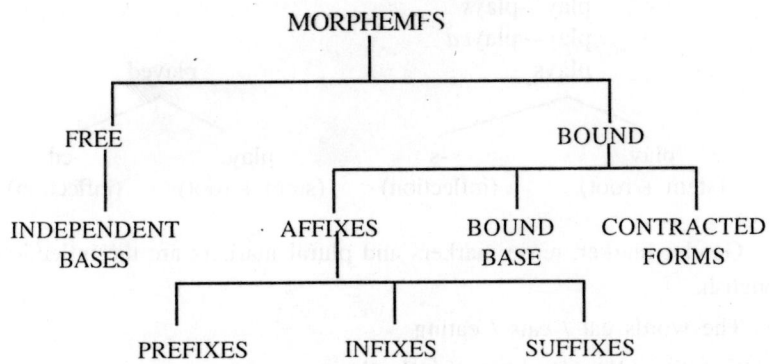

(**A basic classification of English morphemes**)

It is not true that all bound morphemes are affixes or bound bases. For example, in English certain words have contracted forms. The word 'will' can occur in two ways:

(i) as 'will' (such as they will come).
(ii) in a contracted from spelled 'll (such as they'll come).

Other contractions in English include's (the contracted form of 'is'); 've (the contracted from of 'have'); 'd (the contracted form of 'would').

Derivation and Inflection—Derivation is a process of affixation. Derivative forms accept the prefixes or suffixes. They are generally open-ended and allow more than one bound morphemes to join. For example.

  Un + happy + ness

Here un– and -ness both are derivational by character when. un- is a prefix and -ness is a suffix.

We must remember another aspect—class-changing or class-maintaining.

  'happy' is Adjective
  'unhappy' is Adjective

Therefore, un– is a class-maintaining derivational prefix. On the other hand, 'happy' is Adjective and 'happiness' is Noun.

Therefore, -ness is a class-changing derivational suffix. So, derivationals can be both class changing and class maintaining.

The forms that allow only one suffix at a time and do not change their class even after affixation are known as inflectional forms.

for example,

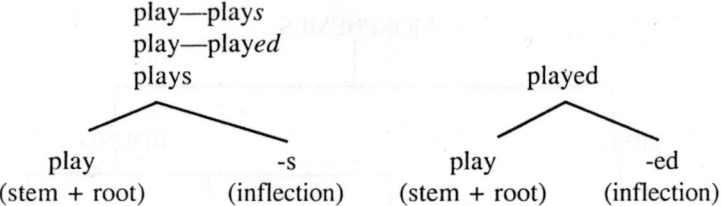

Gender marker, tense markers and plural markers are the inflections of English.

The words eat / eats / eating

Constitute the paradigm of inflection.

Adjective inflectional suffixes :

(a) Comparative marker '–er'—fast–faster

Trilok is faster than Tapan.

(b) Superlative marker '–est'—fast–fastest

Malati is fastest.

Morphological analysis—Consider 'nationalisation'. There are three suffixes attached to the stem 'nation.' At each stage of affixation there is an accompanying category change.

nation + al → national
(n)   (adj.)

national + ise → natinalise
(adj.)   (vb.)

nationalise + ation → nationalisation
(vb.)   (n)

When we are to analyse the morphological structure of 'nationalisation' we follow technique :

ANALYSIS OF MORPHOLOGICAL STRUCTURE

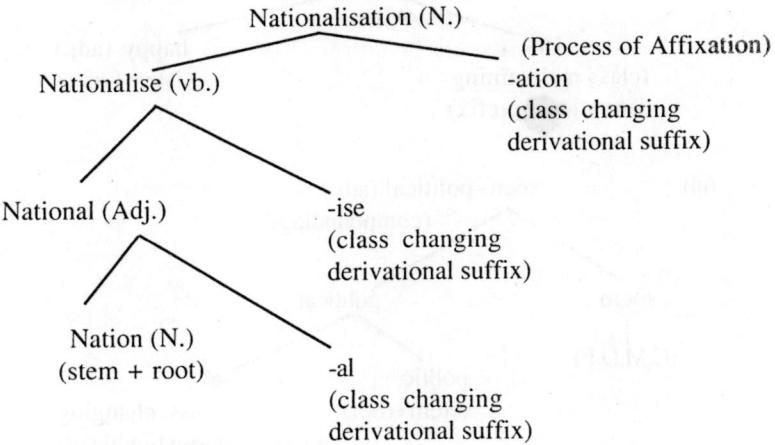

Take another example, 'Characteristics'.

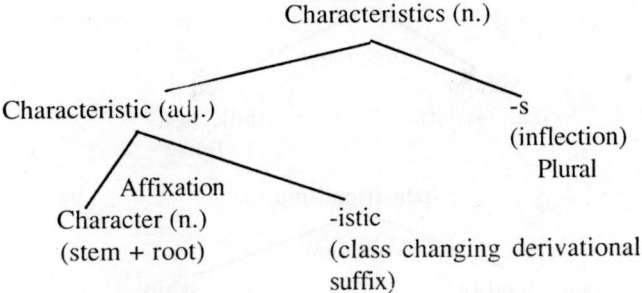

More examples are worked out below :

(i)

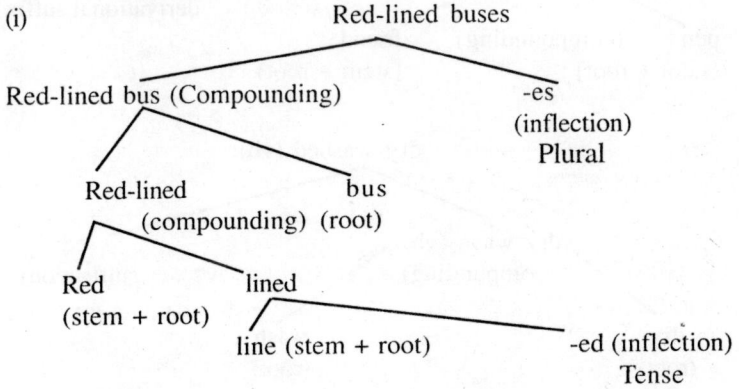

(ii)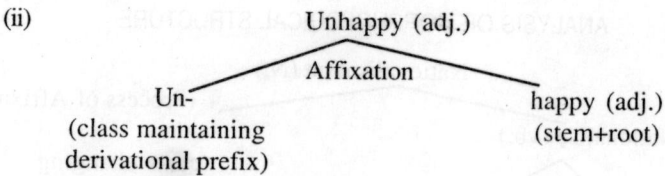

(iii)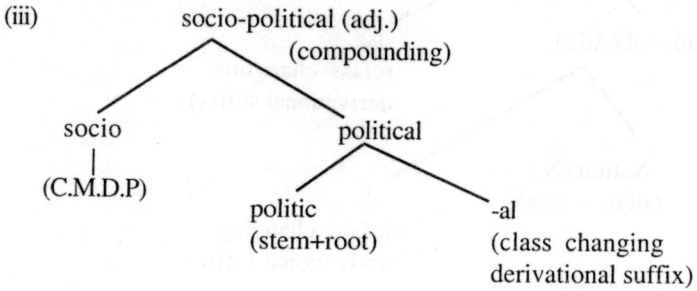

(iv)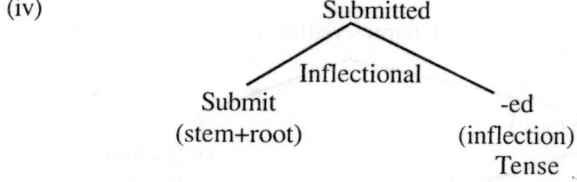

(v)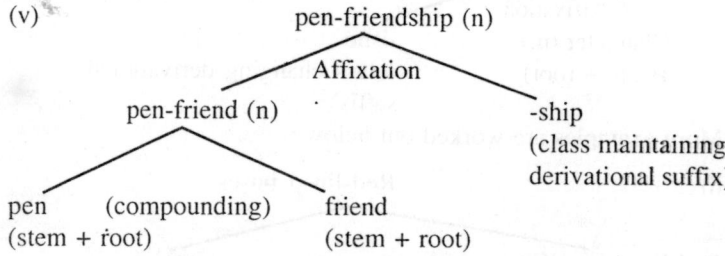

(vi)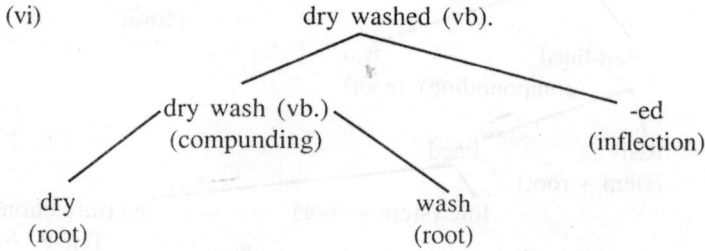

Morphology

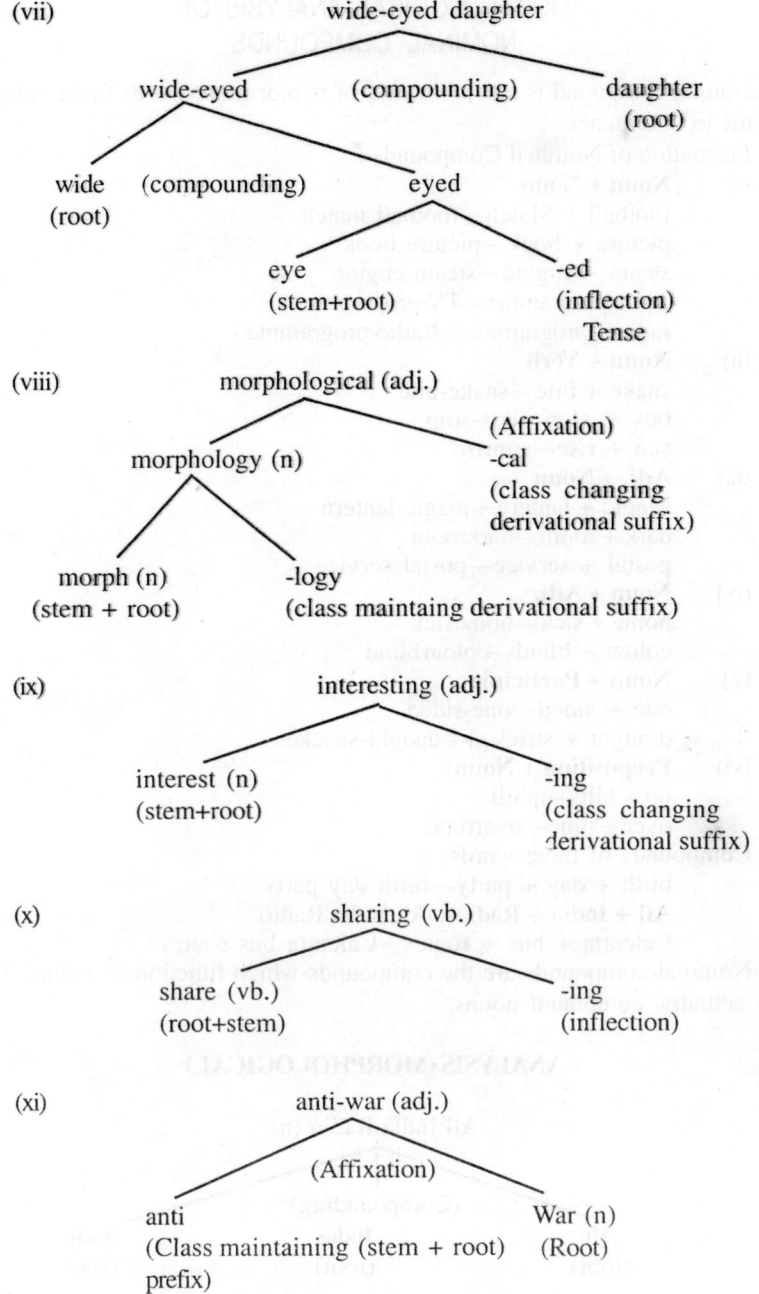

MORPHOLOGICAL ANALYSIS OF NOMINAL COMPOUNDS

A nominal compound is a combination of two or more words functioning as a unit in a sentence.

Formation of Nominal Compounds :
- (i) **Noun + Noun**
  football + Match—football match
  picture + book—picture book
  steam + engine—steam-engine
  TV + programme—TV programme
  radio + programme—Radio programme
- (ii) **Noun + Verb**
  snake + bite—snake-bite
  bus + stop—bus-stop
  sun + rise—sunrise
- (iii) **Adj. + Noun**
  Magic + lantern—magic lantern
  dark + room—darkroom
  postal + service—postal service
- (iv) **Noun + Adj.**
  home + sick—homesick
  colour + blind—colourblind
- (v) **Noun + Participle**
  one + sided—one-sided
  draught + stricken—daught-stricken
- (vi) **Preposition + Noun:**
  up + hill—uphill
  over + time—overtime

Compounds of three words:
  birth + day + party—birth day party
  All + India + Radio—All India Radio
  Calcutta + bus + routes—Calcutta bus routes

Nominal compounds are the compounds which function as nouns. They are actually, compound nouns.

ANALYSIS (MORPHOLOGICAL)

All India Radio (n)

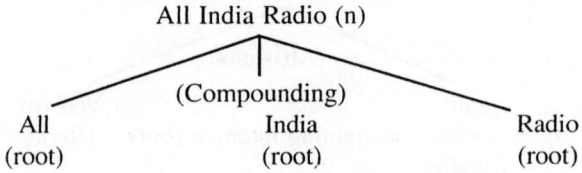

(Compounding)

All   India   Radio
(root)   (root)   (root)

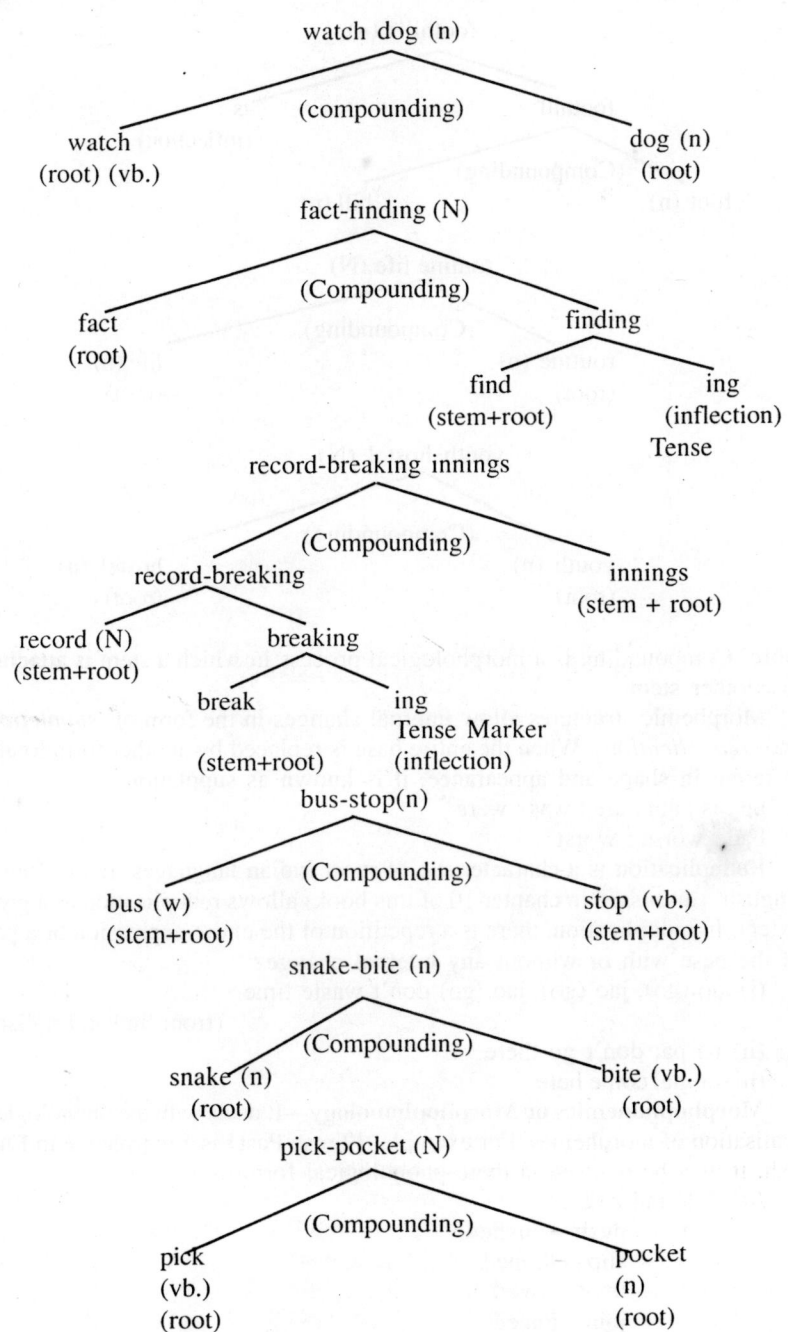

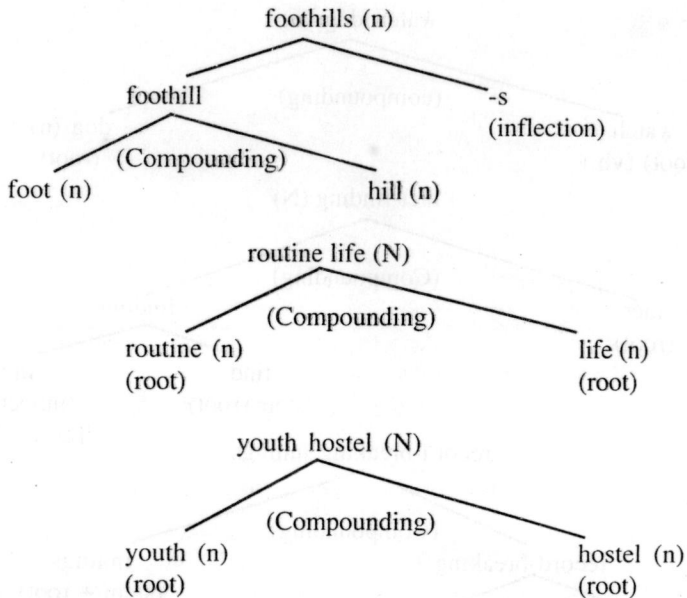

Note: Compounding is a morphological process in which a stem is attached to another stem.

Morphemic structures allow internal changes in the form of *'suppletion'* and *'reduplication'*. When the entire base is replaced by another form totally different in shape and appearance, it is known as suppletion:
 be : is : am : are : was : were
 bad : worse : worst

Reduplication is a characteristic of most Indian languages. Even 'Indian English' (discussed in chapter 10 of this book) allows reduplication to a great extent. In reduplication, there is a repetition of the entire expression or a part of the base with or without any internal change :
 (i) ajo (go), jao (go), jao (go) don't waste time

(from 'Indian English')
 (ii) pa pa; don't go there
 (iii) come, come here

Morphophonemics or Morphophonology—It deals with the phonological realisation of morphemes. For example. {Tense Past} is a morpheme in English. It may be realised in there phonological forms—
 /-t/, /-d/ and /-id/ :
  /-t/ :— push—pushed
      slip—slipped
  /-d/ :— love—loved
      join—joined

/-id/ :— want—wanted
wait—waited

Morphology puts the stem and affix together, and then rules of phonology apply to that. Morphophonemics refers to this phenomenon :
In + probable = improbable
Here / n/ becomes /m/
In + possible + impossible
Here /n/ becomes /m/

When morphemes are combined with the neighbouring phonemes become phonologically more like each other. In the above examples /n/ becomes /m/ under the strong influence of /p/. Nasal sound /n/ changed to /m/ when followed by a bilabial /p/. But we must not forget that in + tangible = intangible.

In this example /n/ remains /n/ because /t/ which follows it is also alveolar. Assimilation, Addition of phoneme, Loss of phoneme and Stress shift are the major morphophonemic processes.

EXERCISES

1. Analyse the morphological structure of the following words. Globalization, socio-cultural, neuro-linguistics, following, recursive, comprehensive, international, non-negative, ungrammatical, transformational, structuralists, understood, anthropologists, blue-eyed monster, mother-tongue interference, self-sacrifice.
2. What is a zero allomorph? Give two examples from English.
3. What is 'bound' and 'free morpheme'. Give suitable examples from English.
4. What is the difference between 'stem' and 'root'?
5. What do you mean by derivation and inflection?
6. Describe the process of affixation in English.
7. What is 'infix'? Give two examples of English 'prefix'.
8. Give two examples of English suffix.

IC ANALYSIS

IC (Immediate Constituent) analysis captures the immediate relationship among the neighbouring constituents. There is a difference between constituency relation and immediate constituency relation. Consider the following sentence:
Fishes live in the sea.
There are five constituents in this sentence. But all of these constituents do not carry equal syntactic load/status. The status of 'fishes' is different from that of 'in'. IC indicates the hierarchical relationship among the neighbouring constituents. In the above example. 'Fishes' is an immediate constituent of 'live in the sea'. After that, 'live' is an IC of 'in the sea'. Then 'in' is the IC of 'the sky' and so on. Immediate relationships among constituents can be captured by bracketing the constituents:

She || is || intelligent

This procedure was orginally set forth by Bloomfield, provided with exegesis by Pike and systematized by Wells. (*Bernard Bloch*)

The aim of IC analysis is to analyze each utterance and each constituent into independent sequences. The ultimate constituents are to be the smallest (possible) meaningful units. Each lower level constituent must be a part of a higher-level items (constituents).

There are five structures in terms of functional interrelation among the constituents :
(i) The structure of Predication
(ii) The structure of Complementation
(iii) The structure of Modification
(iv) The structure of Subordination
(v) The structure of Coordination
Now let us discuss the structures one by one

The Structure of Predication

While doing the structure of Predication we follow the method of 'binary cuts' to arrive at the level of immediate relationships between the subject and the predicate of the sentence. For example,

(i)   He || became a cricketer.
       Subj.   Pred.

(ii)   R.K. Narayan || died.
       Subj.   Pred.

IC Analysis

(iii) I || asked my students to study Grammar.
      Subj.   Pred.

(iv) Sutopa || loves Anirban.
      Subj.   Pred.

(v) 'Modern Linguistics' || is a textbook with a difference.
            Subj.   Pred.

The Structure of Complementation

A Complement is an element without which the sentence/utterance remains incomplete. In this structure of IC, we cut and label the constituents as 'Verbal' and 'Complement'. Let us examine the following examples:

(i)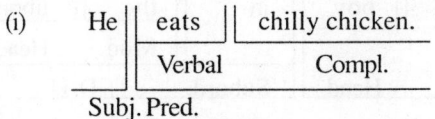

(ii)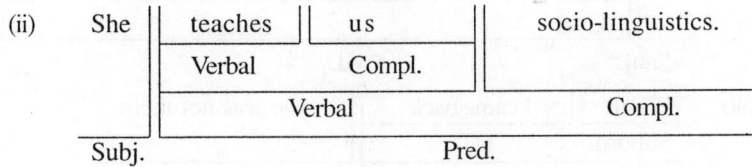

The Structure of Modification

Here the two immediate constitutents are 'Head' and 'Modifier'. Let us consider the following examples :

(i)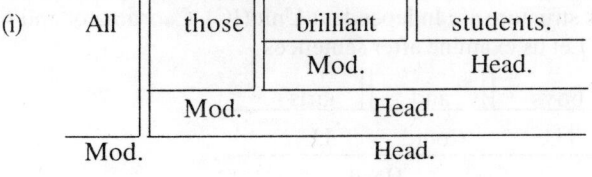

(ii)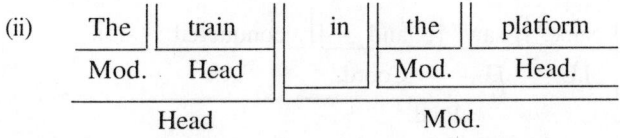

(iii)

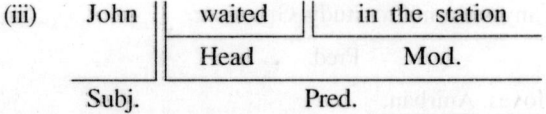

John	waited	in the station
	Head	Mod.
Subj.	Pred.	

The Structure of Subordination

In the structure the cuts are named as the 'Subordinator' and 'Dependent Unit' (D.U.). Consider the following example :

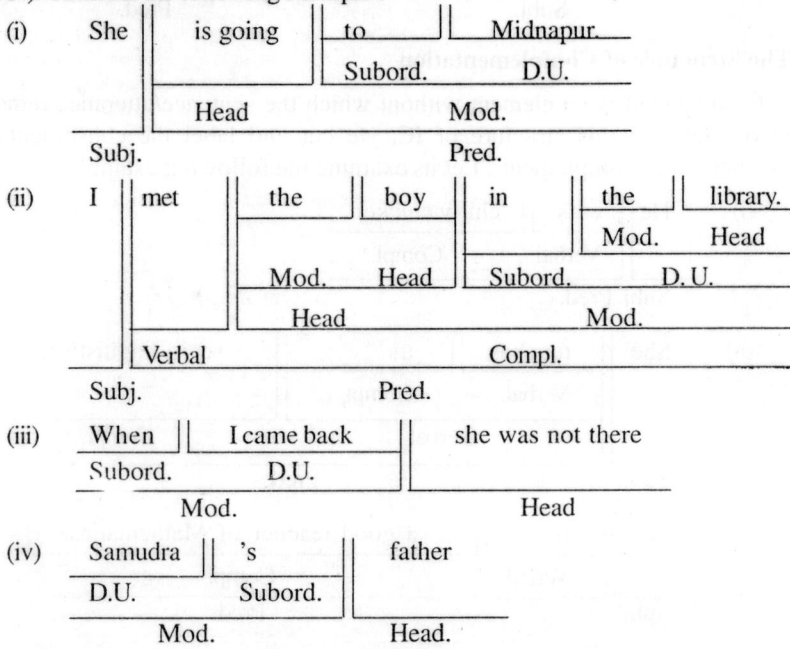

(i) She | is going | to | Midnapur.
         | | Subord. | D.U.
         | Head | Mod.
Subj.   Pred.

(ii) I | met | the | boy | in | the | library.
                                Mod. Head
                  Mod. Head Subord. D.U.
                  Head   Mod.
       Verbal   Compl.
Subj.   Pred.

(iii) When | I came back | she was not there
      Subord.   D.U.
           Mod.   Head

(iv) Samudra | 's | father
      D.U.   Subord.
           Mod.   Head.

(Generally, Possessive('s) and Prepositions are Subordinators)

The Structure of Coordination

This is the only case in IC analysis where the cut is not binary. The elements (immediate) in this structure are Independent Unit (IC), Coordinator and Independent Unit (IC). Let us examine after sentences

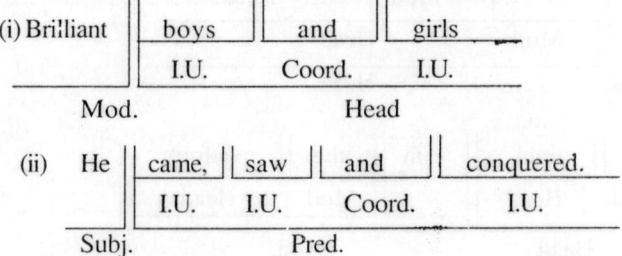

(i) Brilliant | boys | and | girls
              | I.U. | Coord. | I.U.
      Mod.   Head

(ii) He | came, | saw | and | conquered.
        | I.U. | I.U.| Coord.| I.U.
Subj.   Pred.

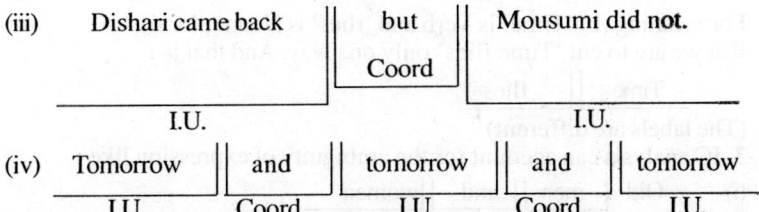

So far we have been discussing non-interrogative sentences. But what will happen to interrogative sentences? Interrogative sentences are the examples of "Discontinuous IC Structures". We may examine the point with some examples :
(i) Is he coming here?
Here the Subject-Auxiliary inversion has taken place. Now we cannot cut (like non-interrogative sentences) and level following the five structures. We have a possible working solution. We can handle the sentence in the following way:
He is coming here.
(After rewriting the sentence in non-interrogative form)

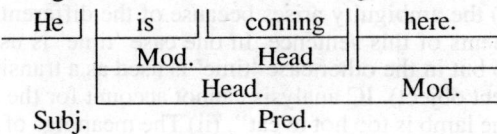

(ii) Is he going to school?
He is going to school.
(After rewriting in the non-interrogative form)

He	is	going	to	school.
	Mod.	Head	Subord.	D.U.
		Head		Mod
Subj.			Pred.	

Limitations of IC analysis:

1. IC analysis fails to indicate the understood elements in a sentence/utterance. For example,
(i) Open the door.
Actually there is 'you' in front of 'open'. This 'you' is implied in the sentence. But there is no way of showing this in IC analysis.
(ii) Go home.
The sentence is "You go home." IC analysis fails to indicate the implied 'you' in the sentence.

2. IC analysis fails to capture the immediate relationships in cases of constructional homonym :
(i) Time flies.
This sentence has two meanings :
(a) Time pases away quickly.
(b) your time flies.
For meaning (a), 'Time' is Noun and 'flies' is Verb.

For meaning (b) 'Time' is Verb and 'flies' is Noun (plural). But we are to cut 'Time flies' only one way. And that is :

    Time || flies

(The labels are different)

3. IC analysis can account for the ambiguity of expression like :

(i)   Old | men || and | women

       Old || man | and | women.

(ii)   Postgraduate || teachers || and || students

      Postgraduate | teachers || and || students

But IC cannot account for certain other types of ambiguities. Examples :
(i) Time flies
(ii) The lamb is too hot to eat.

For sentence (i) the ambiguity arises because of the different levels to the immediate constituents of this sentence. In one case 'time' is used as a noun and 'files' is a verb but in the other case 'time' is used as a transitive verb and 'flies' is noun (direct object). IC analysis cannot account for the ambiguity of sentences like, "The lamb is too hot to eat". (ii) The meanings of this sentence are :

(a) The lamb is very hot it can not eat.
(b) Someone cannot eat the lamb as the lamb is very hot.

There is no scope to capture the ambiguity underlying in these sentences through IC analysis. IC analysis is intended to account for the surface structure of sentences. It cannot give the deep structure realities of the sentences. Its technique of analysis may now seem back-dated in view of modern developments that have taken place in linguistic and specially in the field of syntax.

4. There are overlapping ICs as in "He has little knowledge of or interest in SAARC literature." In this example the word 'little' should be assigned both to "knowledge of SAARC literature" and 'interest in SAARC literature'. IC analysis cannot account for the above overlapping ICs.

EXERCISES

1. Indicate the IC structure of the following sentences or utterances:

(a) Language is both an individual and social phenomena. (b) Culture represents the complete life-ways of the society. (c) I met Kaberi in the library. (d) Defoe is the father of the English novel. (e) The poll outcome in West Bengal is good for industry. (f) He teaches us Linguistics and Phonetics. (g) When she had gone there, I come back. (h) Raju's sister. (i) Bakha is a member of the lowest caste in India. (j) He became a linguist.

2. What is IC alalysis? What are the objectives of IC analysis?
3. What are the limitations of IC analysis?

PHRASES & CLAUSES

Read the following sentences carefully:
(i) I shot an arrow *into the air.*
(ii) I met him *in the Foreign Languages Building.*
(iii) A brilliant boy *with long curling hair* came yesterday.

The groups of words in italics (and underlined) make senses, but not a complete sense. They are not containing a finite verb, but are being used as a single part of speech. They are called phrases. So phrases are a group of words which work together as a unit to perform a single function, to fill one of the positions in a sentence pattern. Phrases may do the functions of different parts of speech. They can be divided broadly into the following classes:

Noun Phrases (NP), Adjective Phrases (Adj. P.), Verbal Phrases (VP), Adverb Phrases (Adv. P.) and Prepositional Phrases (Prep. O or P.P.).

Clauses

Phrases are different from the Clauses. Clauses are groups of words which function as a part of a sentence and which have a Subject and a Predicate.
Examples : (i) Tell me *when will she come.*
(ii) I know Chaman Nahal *who wrote 'Asadi'.*
(iii) *If you make a promise,* you should keep it.
In sentence (i) "When will she come" is a clause.
In sentence (ii) "Who wrote it" is a clause.
In sentence (iii) "If you make a promise" is a clause.
There are three kinds of subordinate clauses :
(i) Noun Clause
(ii) Adjective Clause or Relative Clause
(iii) Adverbial Clause.

Examples

Noun Clause: (i) Pay attention to *what your teacher says.* (ii) They want to know *what was wrong with the fan.*
Relative Clause: (i) I know the man *who lives at Chunripara, Krishnanagar.* (ii) Can you tell me the time *when you will be free.*
Adverbial Clause : (i) She waited for me *until I arrived.* (ii) *As the Sun came out,* everything look 'smiling'.

Linguists use (generally) **Tree diagrams** to represent the structural descriptions of words / sentences. The figures look like branching of trees. Therefore, it is known as **Tree diagram.**

NOUN PHRASE

Consider the following example :

<u>A girl</u> <u>went to school.</u>
 NP   VP

A simple sentence usually consists of a noun phrase and a verb phrase. The same sentence can be labelled by bracketing :

[[a girl   ]   [went to school   ]   ]
S   NP   VP

The commonest way of representing the constituents of a phrase or sentence is to use a tree diagram :

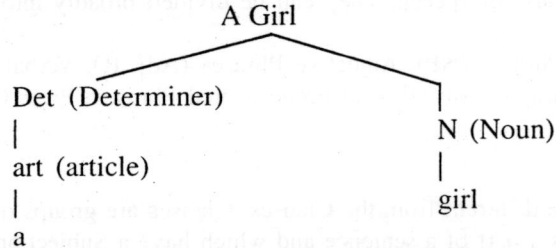

Tree diagrams are used to show how the phrase and the sentence structures are tied together. The analysis looks like that of a tree with branches spreading out from 'nodes'. The elements hang from different branches giving the shape of fruits and flowers.

Constituents of a Noun Phrase (NP)

Noun phrase is a phrase where the Head is a noun. In this phrase the <u>Head Noun</u> is accompanied by <u>Determiners</u>. Modifiers (both premodifiers of postmodifiers). The entire phrase works as a noun.

1. A noun phrase may have only one constituent : only a 'Noun'.

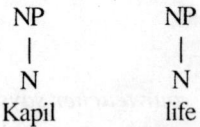

2. A noun phrase may have a 'Det' and a 'Noun' :

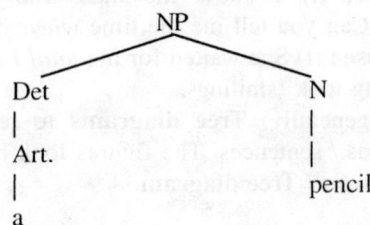

Phrases & Clauses

3. A noun phrase may have 'Det', 'Adj. Phr.' & 'N' :

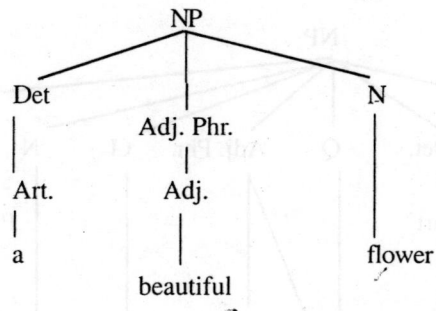

4. A noun phrase may have 'Det', 'Ord.', 'Q' (Quantifier), N :

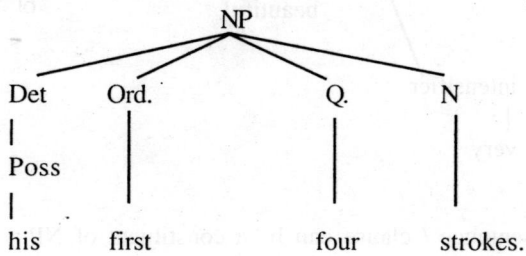

5. The constituents can be 'Det', 'Adj. Phr.', 'NP' & 'N' :

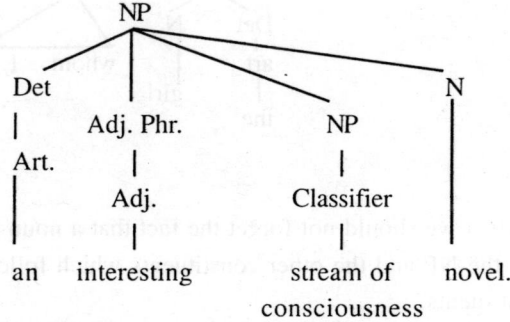

(You may branch classifier from the Head NP itself)

6. The constituents can be even larger in number:
'Pre-det', 'det', 'Q', 'Adj. Phr.', 'Classifier', 'N' and 'PP'

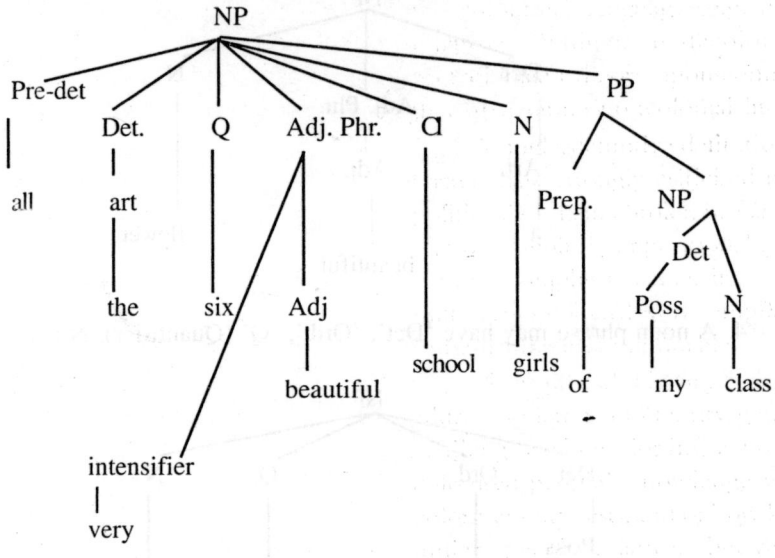

7. A sentence / clause can be a constituent of NP :

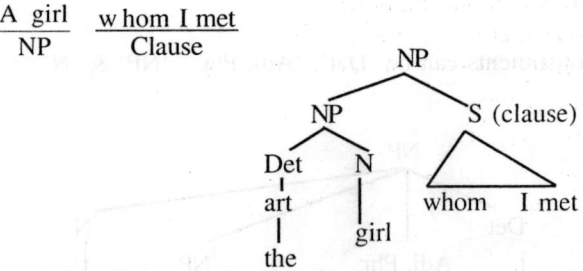

In this context we should not forget the fact that a noun is an obligatory constituent of the NP and the other constituents which follow the noun are optional constituents.

The simple expansion of NP can be represented in the following way :

Phrases & Clauses

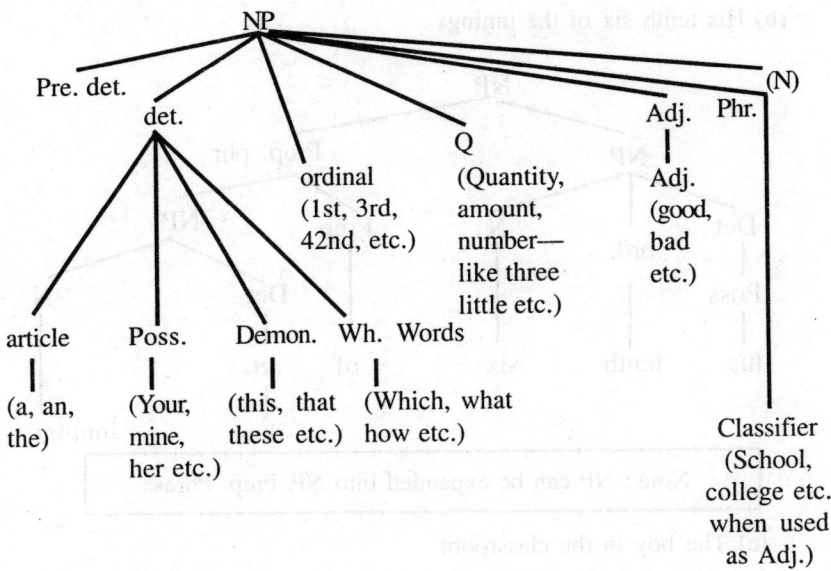

Some examples:

(a) His father's knife

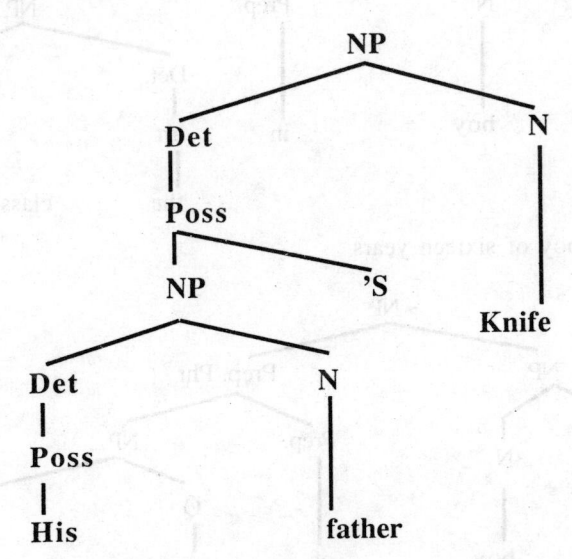

(b) His tenth six of the innings

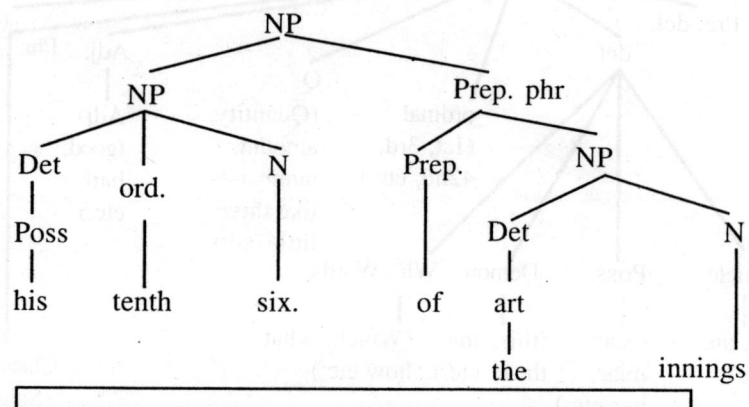

Note : NP can be expanded into NP, Prep. Phrase.

(c) The boy in the classroom

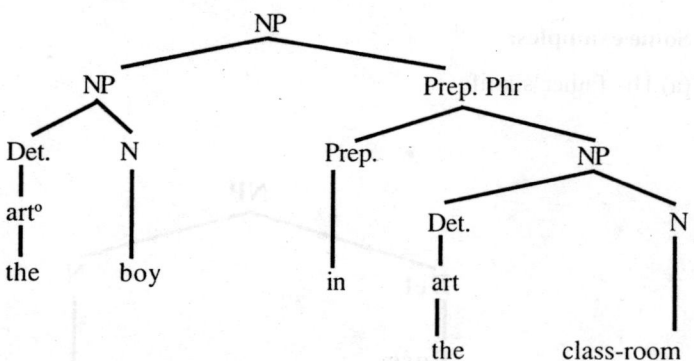

(d) A boy of sixteen years

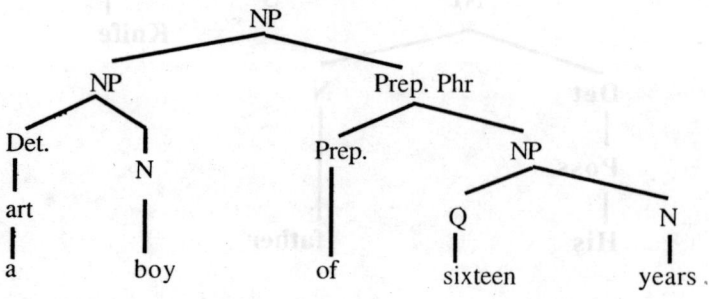

(e) Some of his excellent strokes

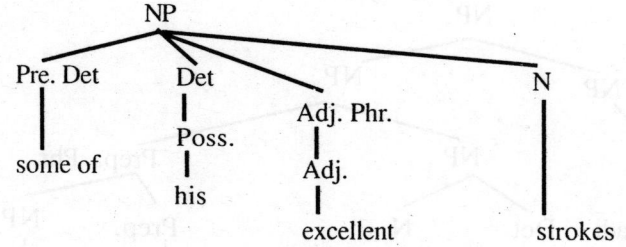

(f) Half of his first fifty very ugly college students.

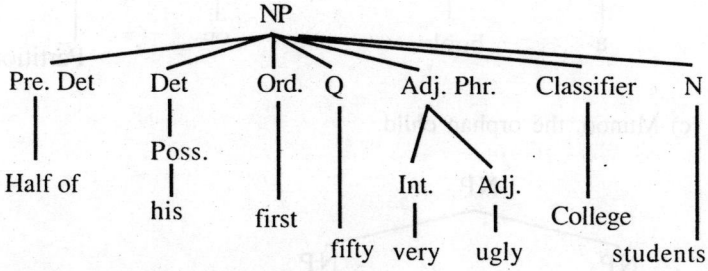

Other possible expansions of NP:

NP can be expanded into NP NP.
Example:
(a) Bakha, a member of the lowest caste in India.

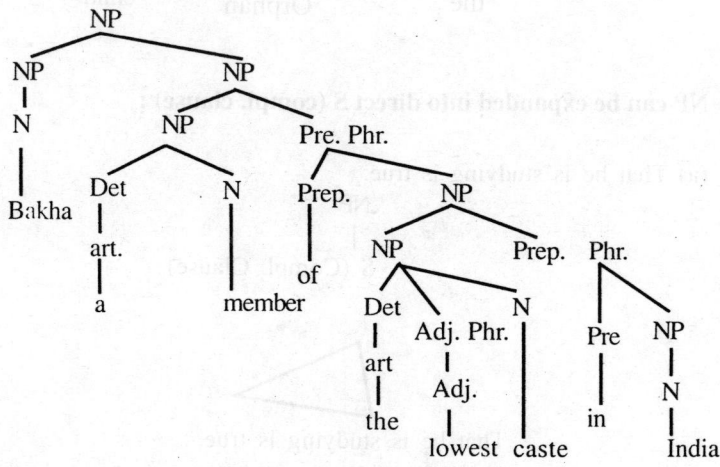

(b) Azadi, a book on partition.

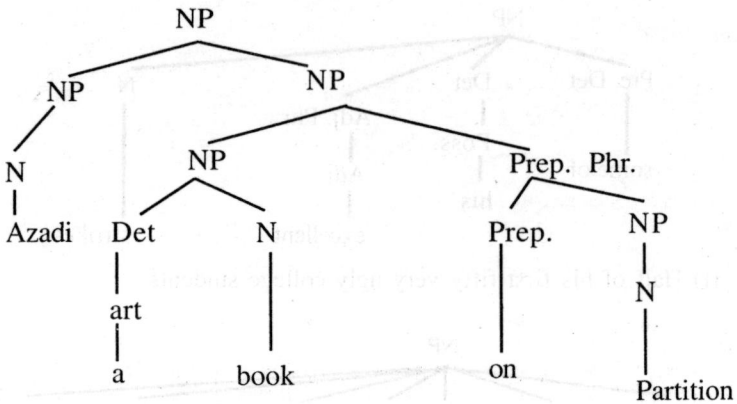

(c) Munoo, the orphan child.

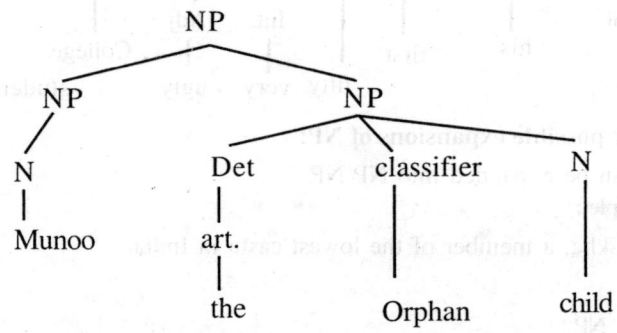

NP can be expanded into direct S (compl. clause) :

(a) That he is studying is true.

NP
|
S (Compl. Clause)

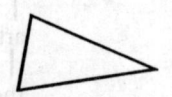

That he is studying is true.

(b) That she is a noble hostess is true.

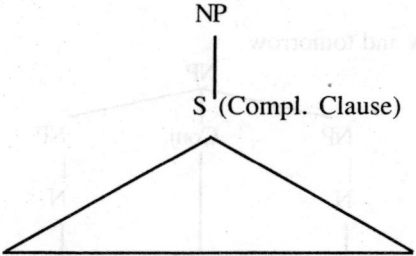

NP can be expanded into NP S :

Examples : (a) A dinner hosted in his honour

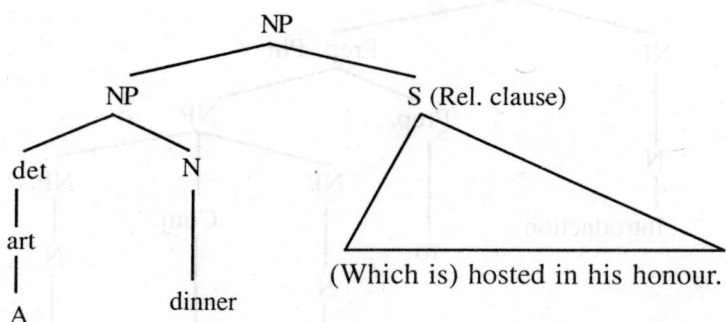

(b) The student whom I met yesterday.

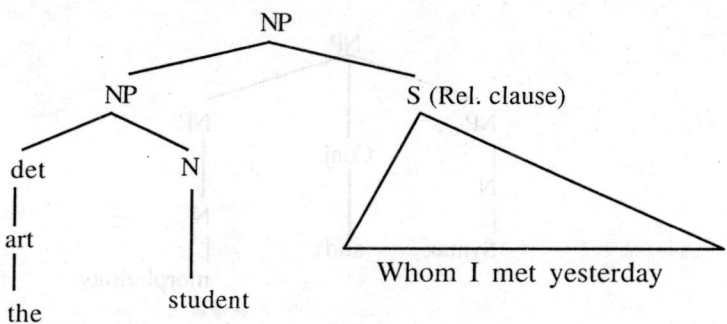

NP can be expanded into NP Conj. NP:

(a) Tomorrow and tomorrow

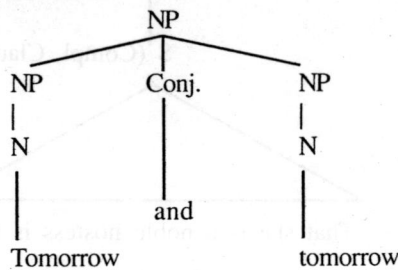

(b) Introduction to Linguistics and ELT

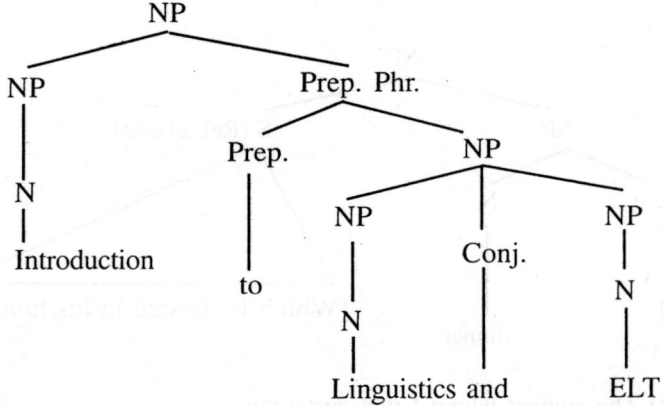

(c) Syntax and morphology

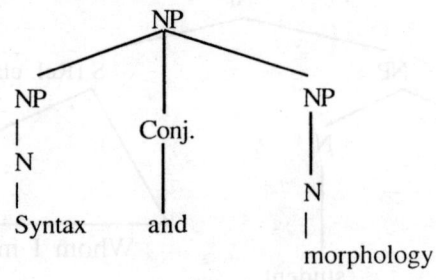

(d) Diagrams and phrase structure rules

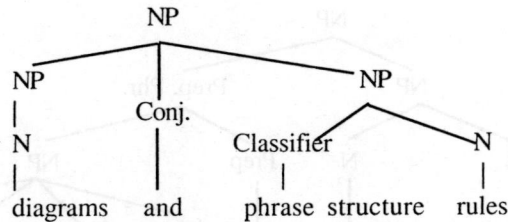

Examples of some NP Structures:
(a) A group of young scientists at the University.

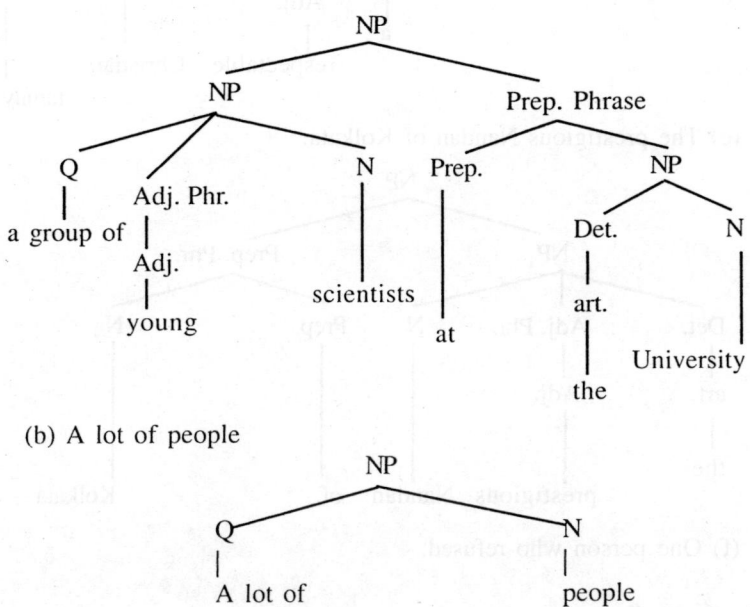

(b) A lot of people

(c) Those little pocket calculators.

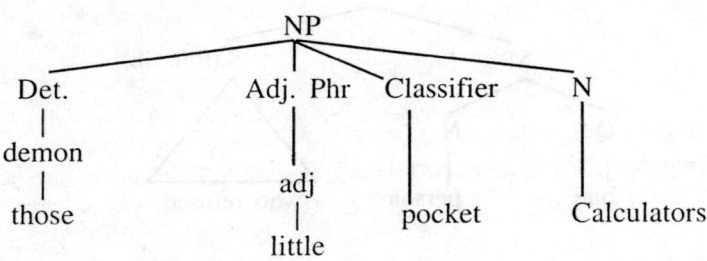

(d) A girl from a respectable Christian family.

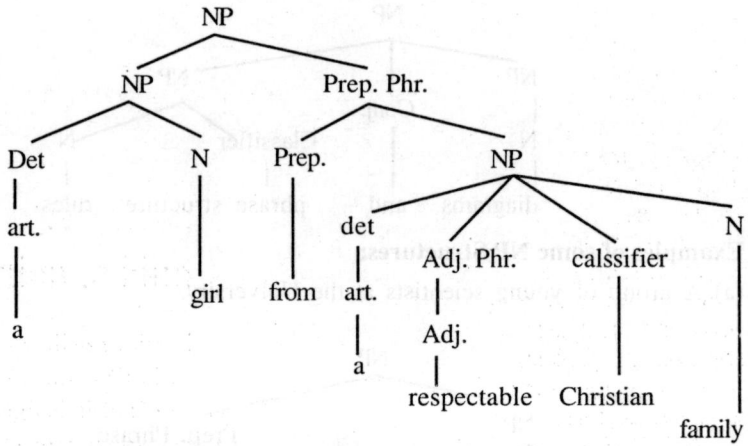

(e) The prestigious Nandan of Kolkata.

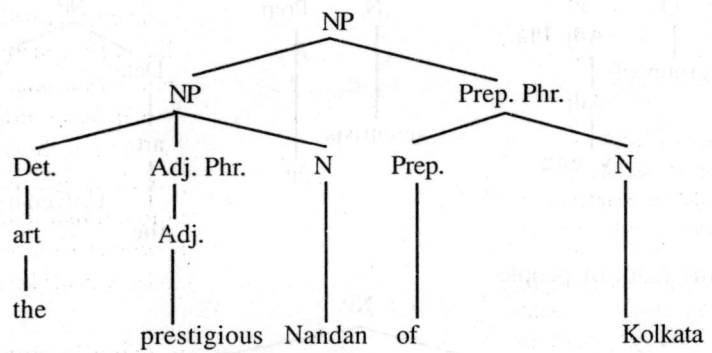

(f) One person who refused.

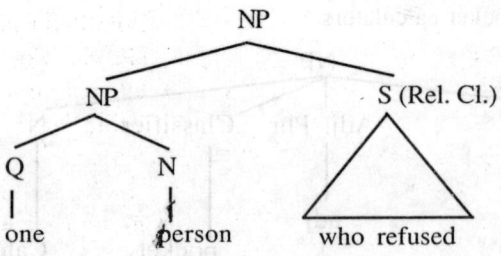

Phrases & Clauses 35

STRUCTURE FOR POSSESSIVE

NP—(Poss) N
Poss— NP Poss—Affix
These rules state that an NP may have an optional possessive phrase preceding the head noun. A Possessive phrase consists of an NP followed by an Affix. It is related/based to/on the property of recursion.

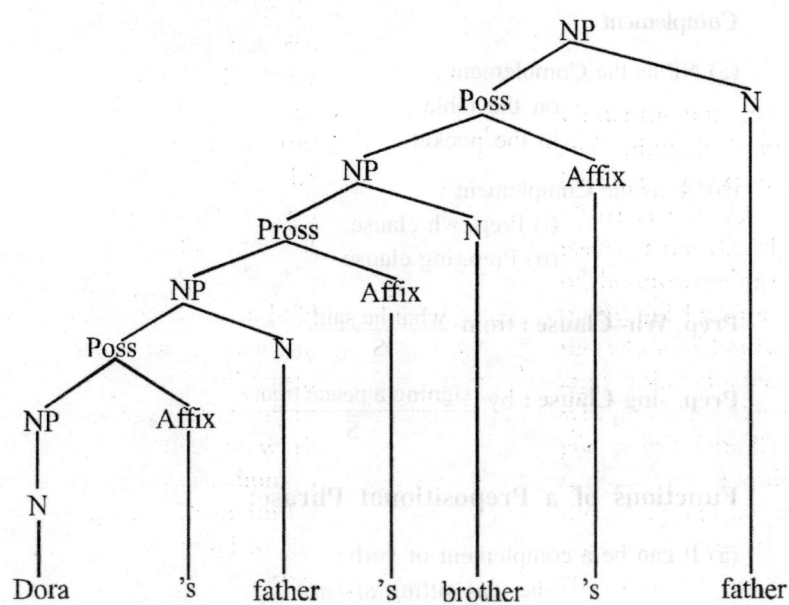

Constituents of a Prepositional Phrase

The possible forms of a Prep Phrase can be like the following :

Examples of simple preposition—Simple prepositions have only one word.

Example : in, on, of, from, upon etc.

Complex preposition—These kinds of prepositions have more than one word.

Example :

types	examples
Adv. + Prep. →	along with,

Prep. + N + Prep. →
1   2

away from,
owing to
in spite of,
in case of,
with respect to

Adj./ /.... can modify a prep :
Right on the top.
exactly on time.

Complement

(a) NP as the Complement :
on the table
in the pocket

(b) S̄ as the Complement :
(i) Prep. wh clause
(ii) Prep. ing clause

Prep. Wh- Clause : from $\underline{\text{what he said}}$
$\phantom{\text{from what he}}\overline{S}$

Prep. -ing Clause : by $\underline{\text{signing a peace treaty.}}$
$\phantom{\text{by signing a peace}}\overline{S}$

Functions of a Prepositional Phrase:

(a) It can be a complement of verb :
She was sitting *at ease*.

(b) It can be a complement of an Adj. :
Proud *of*
fond *of*

(c) It can be a complement of a Noun :
a piece of *cloth*.

(d) It can be used as an Adjective :
I saw Prabir *in the library*.
I met Joyjit *at the Howrah Station*.

Phrases & Clauses

Prepositional phrase can also consist of a Preposition and another Prepositional phrase : From behind the window :

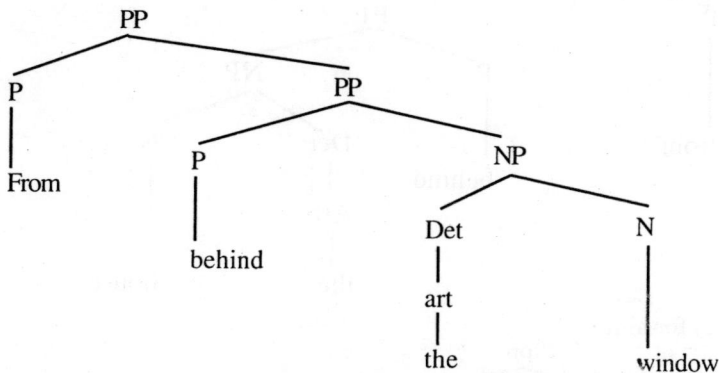

Disguise Preposition : Disguise prepositions are prepositions which don't look like the prepositions but actually function as prepositions. They are structurally prepositions:

(a) I shall go there at <u>7 o'clock.</u>
    (of clock)

(b) Sumit is sitting <u>be-hind</u> me.
    (by hind)

In (a) and (b) 'of' and 'by' respectively are the prepositions in disguise.

Analysis of Some Prep. Phrases:

(a) in the school hours.

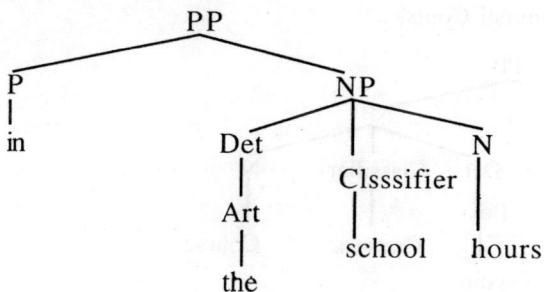

(b) from behind the house.

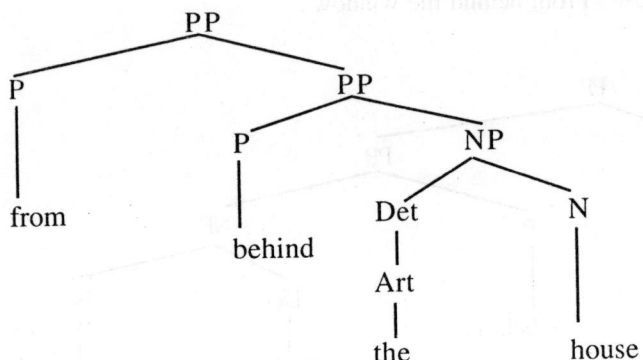

(c) for him.

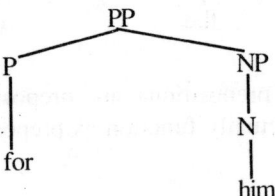

(d) near the Govt. College.

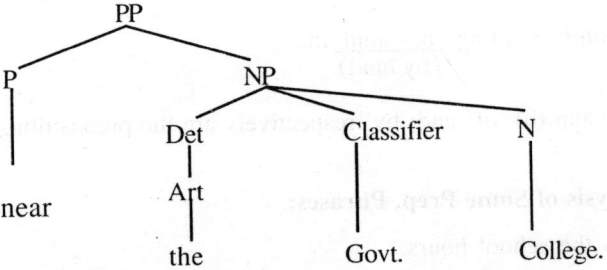

(e) by your Grammar Course

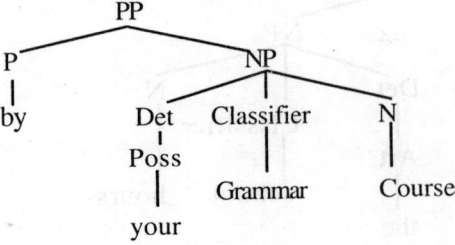

Constituents of an Adjective Phrase:
These Phrases have Adjective as the head :

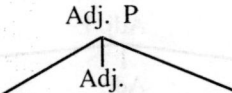

(a) An adjective phrase may consist of only an adjective :

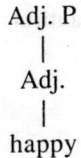

Adj. P
|
Adj.
|
happy

(b) An adjective phrase may consist of an adj. and PP :

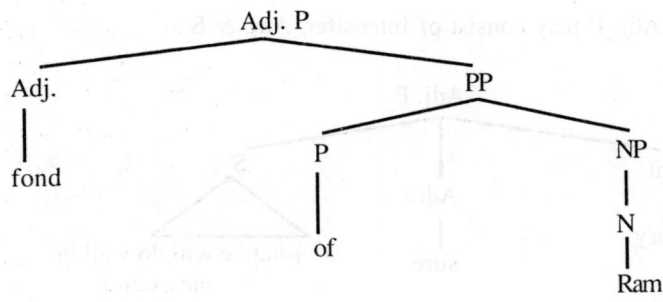

(c) Adj. P may consist of intensifier & Adj.

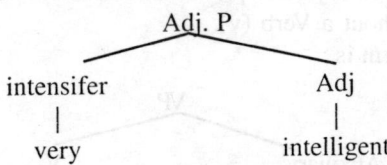

(d) Adj. P may consist of Adv. P & Adj. :

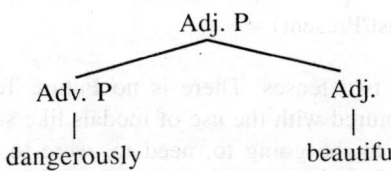

(e) Adj. P may consist of Adv. P, Adj. & complement.

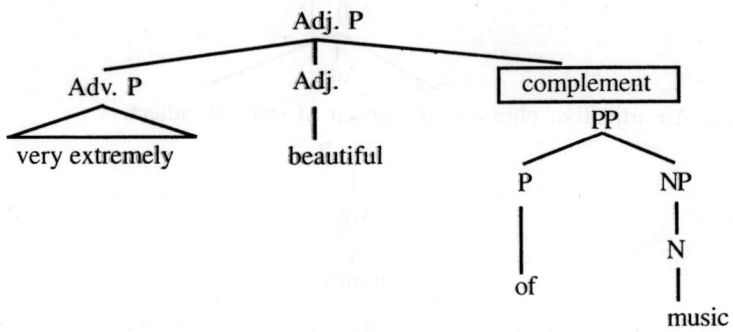

(f) Adj. P may consist of Intensifer, Adj. & S :

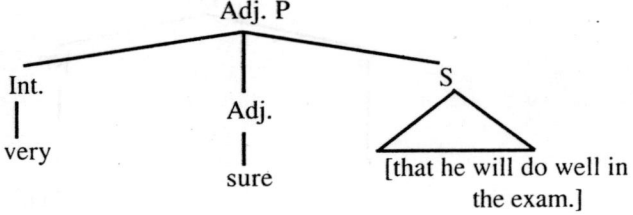

The Constituents of a Verb phrase (VP) :

There can not be an adjective phrase without an adjective; similarly, there cannot be a VP without a Verb (v).

The basic VP form is :

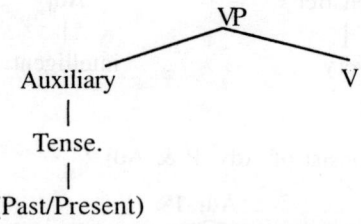

English has only two tenses. There is no Future Tense in English. In English, future is captured with the use of modals like shall, will, can, may, should, would, have to, be going to, need to, were to, etc. These modals (modal auxiliaries) refer to 'possible worlds'. For example :

(a) I shall go there.
    Here 'shall' denotes future desire/possibility.
(b) I can do it.
    Here 'can' refers to the 'ability'.
(c) It may rain tomorrow.
    Here 'may' denotes future possibility.

Modals express subjective attitudes like permission, ability, probability, possibility, willingness, desire, necessity, assurance, etc. Two modals cannot be used together.

Auxiliary (helping verb) consists of the following items :

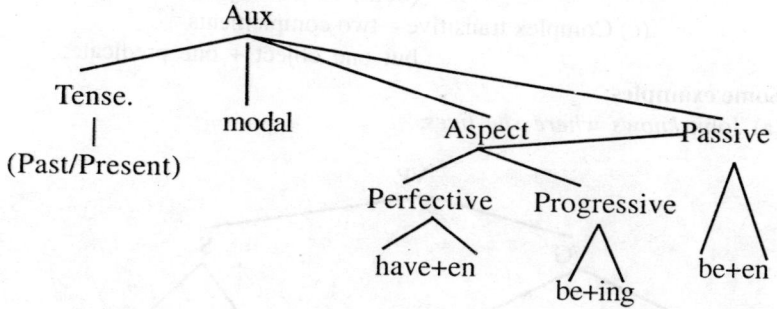

Example :
    may have been teaching
    Here the Aux. consists of the following :

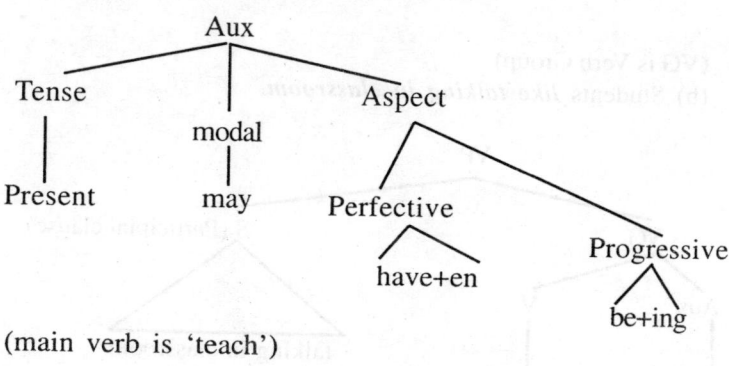

(main verb is 'teach')

VP can be expanded into the following :

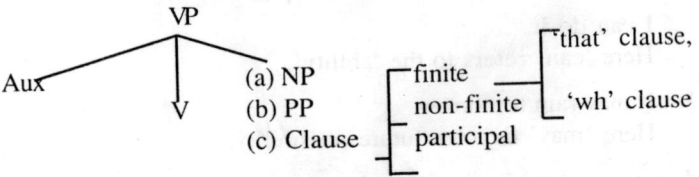

English verbs can be of two types (i) Transitive, (ii) Intransitive. Transitive verbs can be of three types :
        (a) Mono transitive—have one complement.
        (b) Distransitive—have two complements
                    (both) of the objects.
        (c) Complex transitive—two complements
                    but one object + one predicate.

Some examples:
(a) John *knows where she lives.*

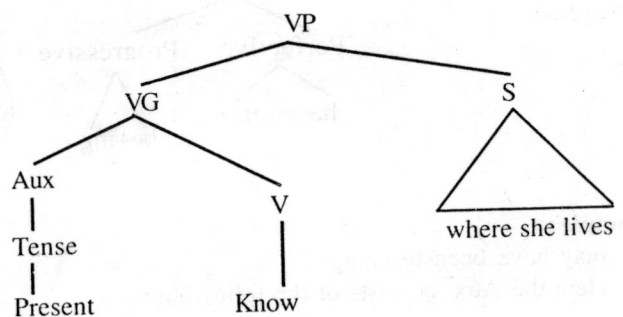

(VG is Verb Group)
(b) Students *like talking in classroom.*

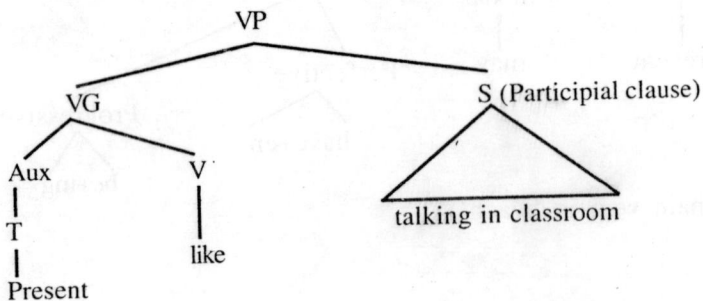

Phrases & Clauses

Ditransitive verbs (like give, buy etc.) take two objects : one **Direct** & one Indirect.

Example :
Samuel gave Meena a flower.

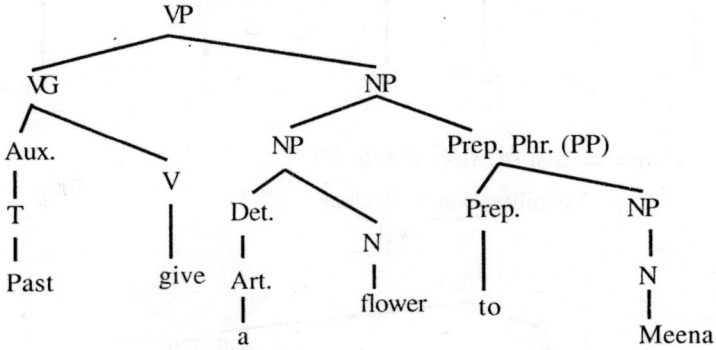

Take another example:

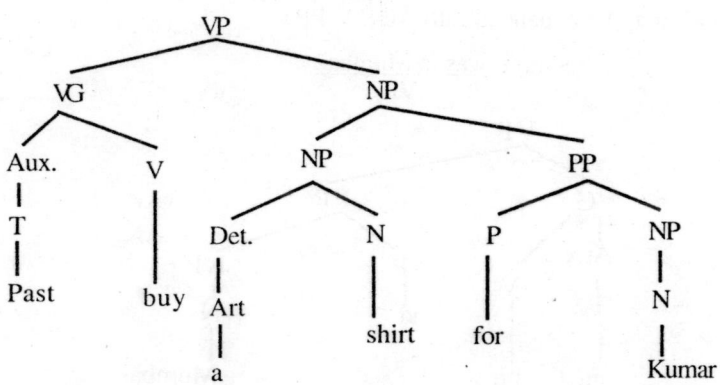

VP may consist of Aux. V. NP NP:

I gave him a novel
       VP

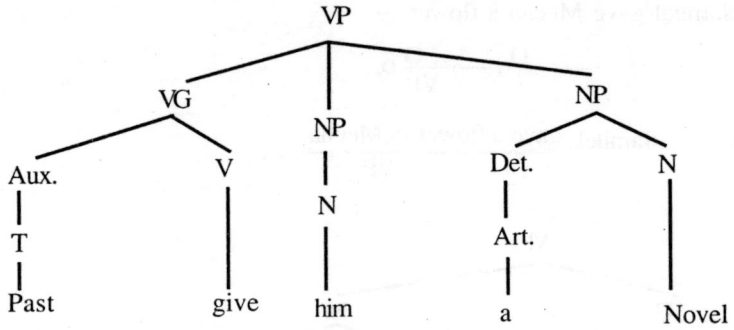

VP may consist of Aux. V Adj. P :

Visibility was very clear.
           VP

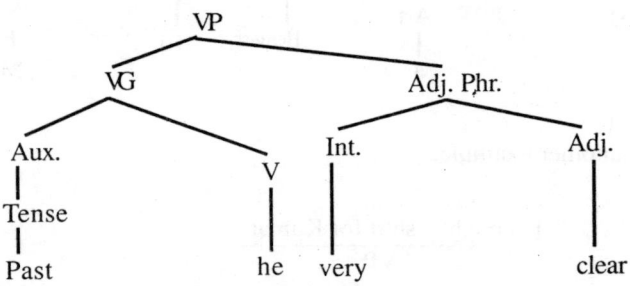

VP may be expanded into Aux. V PP :

Surajit was in Mumbai.
         VP

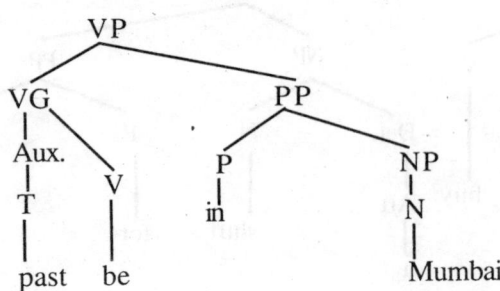

Phrases & Clauses

(a) VP may consist of Aux, V, NP, Adv. P. too :

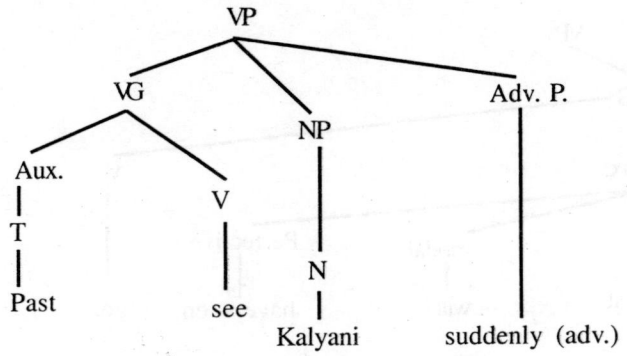

(b) I $\dfrac{\text{saw Kalyani suddenly.}}{\text{VP}}$

I $\dfrac{\text{miss him terribly.}}{\text{VP}}$

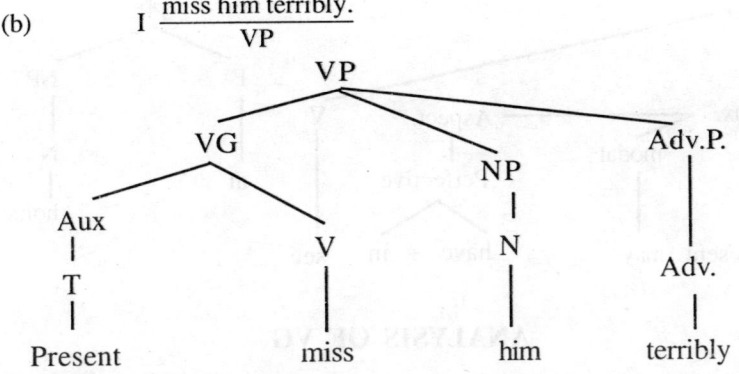

(a) Some examples of VP and their structures :
   Were to occur

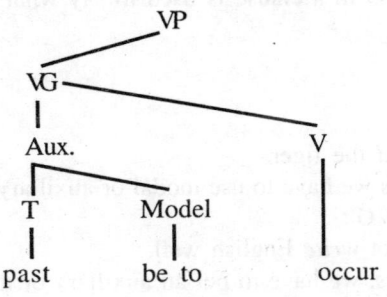

(b) Would have gone.

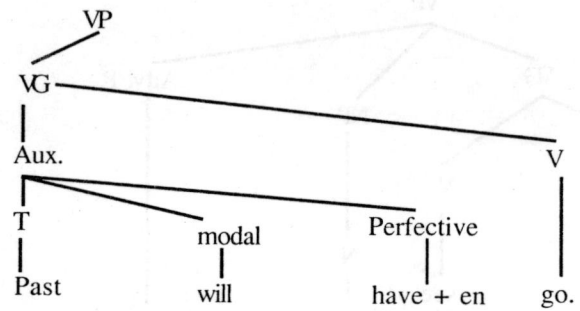

(c) may have seen at home.

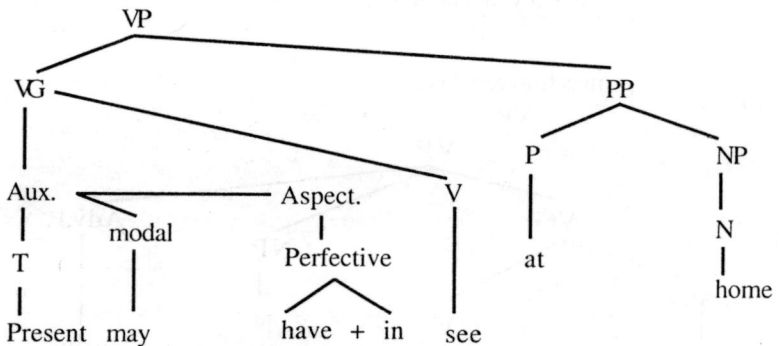

ANALYSIS OF VG

In a clause the VG usually comes after the subject and always has a main verb. The main verb has several forms. The VG changes in negative clauses and questions. The VG in a clause is used to say what is happening in an action or situation.

Examples :
    I *waited.*
    They *killed* the tiger.

In negative clauses we have to use modal or auxiliary and put 'not' after the first word of the VG :
    He does not *write* English well.

In yes/no questions, we have to put an auxiliary or modal first, then the subject, then the rest VG :

Did you *meet* Ranjana?
Some VGs have an object or two objects after then.

(a) Have been learning

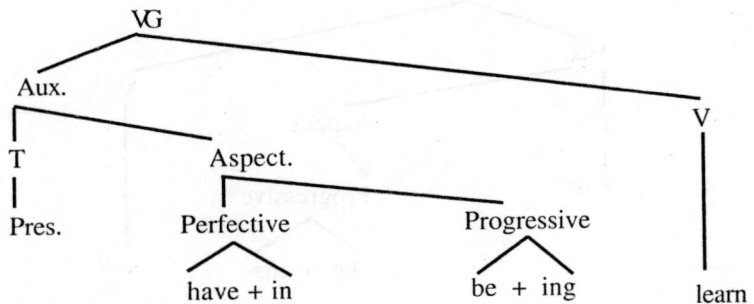

(b) Was done

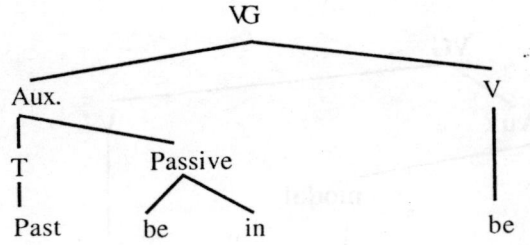

(c) Has been sleeping

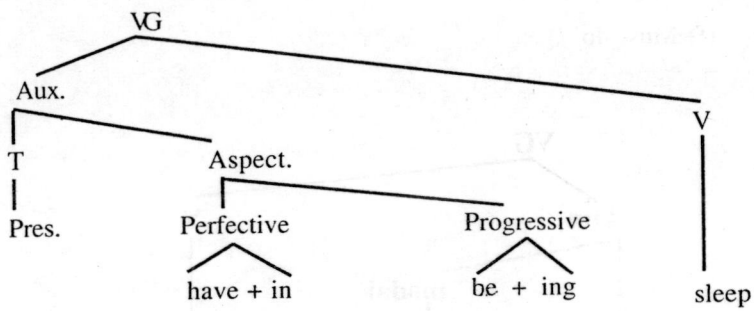

(d) Was crying

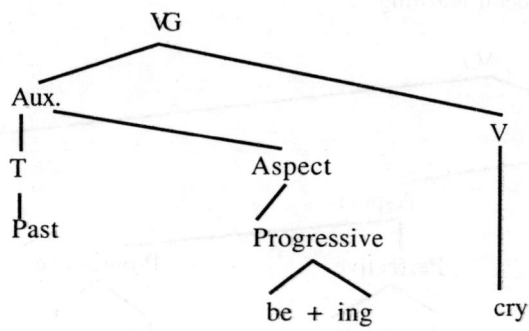

(e) Shall go

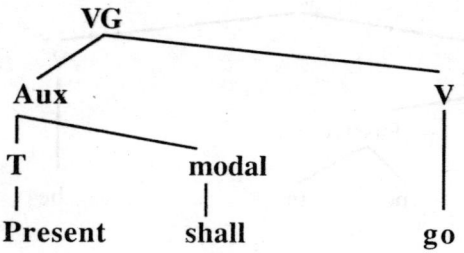

(f) Must do

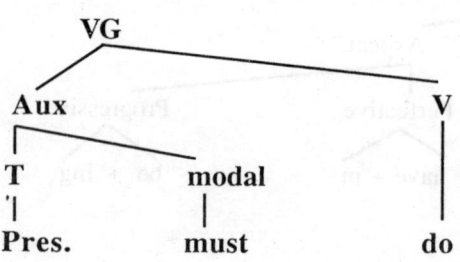

(g) Has been running

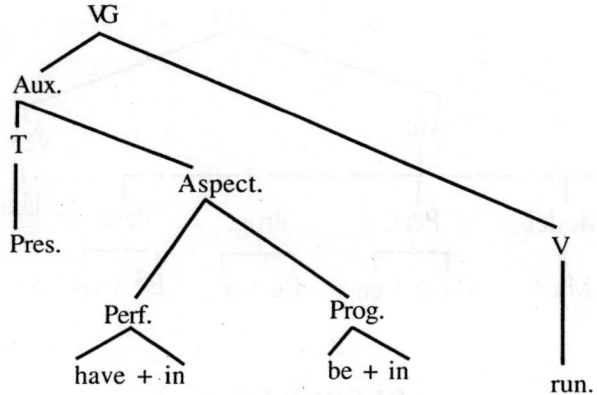

(h) Called for

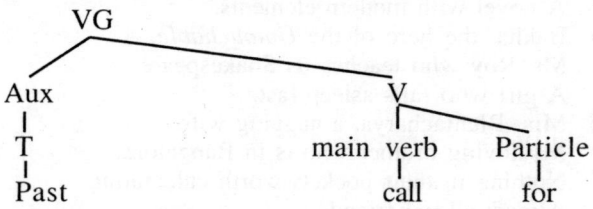

i) Might have been saying

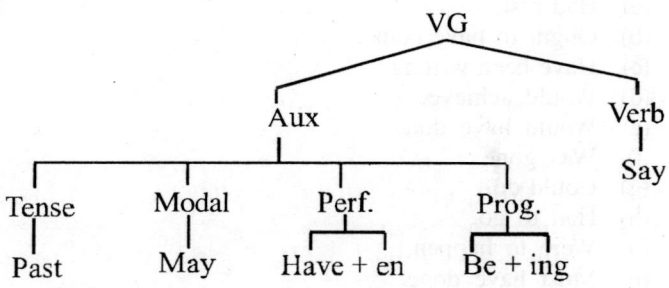

(j) Must have been being understood.

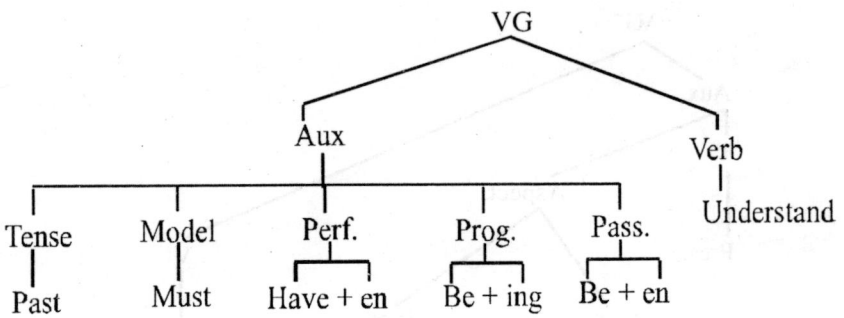

EXERCISES

1. **Analyse the following NPs :**
   (a) First three very intelligent very ugly wives.
   (b) Life that is precious.
   (c) A novel with modern elements.
   (d) Bakha, the hero of the *Untouchable*.
   (e) Mr. Roy who teaches us Shakespeare.
   (f) A girl who falls asleep fast.
   (g) Mrs. Bhattacharya, a nagging wife.
   (h) My loving brother who is in Bangalore.
   (i) Nothing in their pockets worth calculating.
   (j) Almost all our friends.
   (k) A brilliant boy from a government school.
   (l) One person who refused to take the responsibility.
   (m) An Important one-day cricket match.

2. **Analyse the following verbal groups:**
   (a) Had rest.
   (b) Ought to have come.
   (c) Have been writing.
   (d) Would achieve.
   (e) Would have done.
   (f) Was gone.
   (g) Could do.
   (h) Had to go.
   (i) Were to happen.
   (j) Must have done.

Phrases & Clauses 51

3. **Analyse the following VPs:**
   (a) Went to Kolkata.
   (b) Had been teaching in a school.
   (c) Has been sleeping in a room.
   (d) Miss her badly.
   (e) Was in his room for some days.
   (f) Knows where he lives.
   (g) Listens to music.
   (h) Shall do what you want.

4. **Analyse the following PPs:**
   (a) From behind the school building.
   (b) In the college hours.
   (c) For her.
   (d) By your grammar teacher.
   (e) For a man who likes to read Rabindranath.
   (f) For a person who likes to draw trees.
   (g) On the floor.
   (h) With the pen I have.
   (i) In the college where I studied.
   (j) In a famous place.
   (k) With the bat.
   (l) In the writings of Karnad.
   (m) In the opening partnership.
   (n) In the playing Australian team.
   (o) On the boundary line.
   (p) In a crowded bus.
   (q) By a man from Tasmania.
   (r) In Mr. Mund's room.
   (s) With creative thoughts.
   (t) For Professor Gutman.

5. **Identify the VGs. Analyse them.**
   We do gratefully remember the support given to us. We have been giving priority to postcolonial writings. We are to publish a special issue on Indian English Poetry. Our mission will be successful if it glorifies both the readers and the writers.

STRUCTURAL LINGUISTICS AND PHONOLOGY

Fardinand de Saussure is considered the 'Father of Modern Linguistics'. *A Course in General Linguistics* is his famous book where his notions about language and linguistics have been expressed. His notions gave a new direction to language study:
(i) Saussure distinguished between diachronic study and synochronic study. A *synchronic study* is a descriptive study of language at a particular point of time. For example, the linguistic study of English of 1990s. A *diachronic study* is the study of language over a long period of time. For example, philological study of language.
(ii) Saussure distinguished between *'signifier'* and *'signified'*. Signifier is a linguistic sign which stands for something 'abstract'. 'Signified' is the thing referred or referent. For example, 'horse' which is a linguistic signifier, refers to the abstract concept of a horse (with special marks of identity).
(iii) Saussure also made a distinction between *langue* and *parole*. The actual linguistic output or utterances produced both in the form of spoken and written are parole. According to Chomsky, parole is 'performance'. The abstract intuition underlying parole is *langue*. The abstract set of conventions and intuition make parole possible- According to chomsky, language is 'competence'.
(iv) Saussure also made a distinction between *'Syntagmatic'* and *'Paradigmatic'*. Actually, both these terms refer to do the relation among the constituents of sentences/utterances. Syntagmatic relation between the constituents of utterances refer to the linear (horizontal) relation among the constituents. For example,
Manu goes to college.
There is a syntagmatic relation between the four words (including one structure/form word 'to') in the above sentence.
Paradigmatic relation is the relation between an element which is present in a sentence and the elements/constituents which are not present in a sentence. It shares mainly a vertical relationship. For example,
    Neha goes to *Indore*. → (1)
    Neha goes to *Bhopal*. → (2)
    Neha goes to *Coimbatore*. → (3)
    Neha goes to *Ujjain*. → (4)
Different items take the above object positions. And the relationship between 'Indore' and 'Bhopal' or 'Coimbatore' or 'Ujjain' are paradigmatic. In sentence one we have Indore which is present in the sentence. 'Bhopal', 'Coimbatore' and 'Ujjain' can take the position of 'Indore.'

American Descriptive Linguistic Approach

This approach is also known as Structural Linguistic Approach. Franz Boas, Edward Saper and Leonard Bloomfield (1887-1948) were the pioneers of this new Approach in linguistics. They looked at language as an expression of the social behaviour. For them, language learning was a matter of habit formation. The structuralists like Bloomfield, believed in the following notions regarding language :

(i) For the structuralists, language was the total output produced in a speech community. So, they believed in parole—the performance part of the language concerned. For them, language was "the totality of utterances made in a speech community".

(ii) The objectives of Structural Linguistics were the identification and classification of linguistic data. They were less interested to form general empirical rules/principles of language.

(iii) Linguistic corpus was used as data for linguistic analysis. Linguistic corpus was the phonetically transcribed version of native speakers speech gathered through 'field study.'

(iv) The structuralists used the technique of 'discovery procedure' as a mode to analyse linguistic systems like phonology, morphology and syntax.

Phonology

The selection of speech sounds and their organization constitute the phonology of the language.

Phone—A phoneme is a minimal distinctive unit in the sound system of a language.

Minimal pair—A minimal pair is a pair of words with difference at the level of any segment (of sound). This difference may cause change in meaning or not. For example,

[bed]
[beg]

'bed' and 'beg' are two different words because of the difference between the words which lies at the last segment. The replacement of sounds at the last segment [g] by [d] is responsible for the change in meaning.

Distribution—It is the context in which an item can occur. Distribution in phonology is the occurrence of a particular sound in an environment.

A Shared Distribution—[p] & [P^h] have different distributions in phonology. [P^h] occurs only in the first segment of stressed syllable, whereas [p] occurs in all other positions (elsewhere) except in the initial position of the stressed syllable. So [p] & [P^h] don't enjoy the shared distribution.

But take the following examples,

a   book   this   book,   my   book.
| N | N | N
art   demon.   poss.

Articles, demonstratives or possesives are in shared distribution because all of them can find a place at one time in a Noun Phrase (NP).

Mutually Exclusive Position—Where one element can occur but the other cannot.

Example,

Clear [1]
and
Dark [1]

Clear [1] is followed by vowel or j/ : [–V /j]
Dark [1] is followed by consonant & word finally :

$$\begin{bmatrix} -C \\ -\# \end{bmatrix}$$

[# is the symbol of word boundary.]

Dark [1] and Clear [1] are the allophones (different realizations of the same phoneme) occur in mutually exclusive positions.

Totally Exhaustive Situation—If two elements are put together and they exhaust all positions they form totally exhaustive situation. For example,

Dark [1] and clear [1] are totally exhaustive.

The Principles of Phonemic Analysis: The principles are used on the phonetic data to find out whether the sounds are allophones of the same phoneme or the sounds are separate phonemes. We have several principles of Phonemic Analysis :

(i) Contrastive Distribution: When two sounds occur in identical environment and one sound is replaced by the other sound and the replacement bring out a change in meaning,—they (the sounds) are said to be in contrastive distribution. In contrastive distribution the sounds occur in minimal pairs (the difference in one segment). When the sounds are in Contrastive Distribution, they are the different phonemes.

(ii) Free Variation: When two sounds occur in indentical environment and the mutual replacement of the sounds do not bring about any change in meaning—they are said to be in Free Variation. For example, the dark [1] and clear [1] are the allophones of [1]. If dark [1] is replaced by clear [1], the meaning of the words do not change. So dark [1] and clear [1] are the allophones of [1]. They are not the different phonemes.

Structural Linguistics and Phonology 55

(iii) Complementary Distribution: Two sounds do not occur in identical environment in this distribution. The sounds should be in mutually exclusive environment (if one sound occurs, the other will never occur in that place).
For example:
(i) [p] and [Pʰ] are in Complementary Distribution in English. [Pʰ] occurs only in the initial position of an accented syllable and [p] never occurs there.

(ii) If the sounds (under study) are in Complementary Distribution we cannot stop at this point only. We need to study the 'Sufficient Phonetic Similarity' of the sounds concerned. We know about the three-term description of the speech sounds. At least two levels (out of three levels) should be similar to say—the sounds under study have sufficiently phonetic similarity.

The 'three-terms' of speech sounds are—
           (i) Voiced/Voiceless
           (ii) Place of articulation
           (iii) Manner of articulation

(iv) Pattern Congruity: The pattern in which sounds are organized, is studied in this principle. We must look into the data to make out a systematic process (related to pattern).

Now let us examine some of the problems
Problem-1 : Study the following data and say whether [k] and [kʰ] are different phonemes or allophones of the same language.

    [kʰIg] = mad   [esem] = class
    [kIg] = mad   [ekem] = you
    [kIld] = pen   [IdIm] = love
    [pIn] = hen

Answer : By studying [kʰIg] = mad and
[kIg] = mad, we can say that—

The replacement of [kʰ] by [k] do not affect the meaning of the word. [kʰIg] constitutes a pair where the difference is only at the initial segment. The sounds [kʰ] and [k] are in Free Variation. Therefore, [kʰ] and [k] are the allophones of the same phoneme.

Problem-2 : Study the following data and say whether [d] and [z] are the allophones of the same phoneme or they are different phonemes.

                DATA
        [din] = sin   (1)
        [kim] = dog   (2)
        [mald] = father   (3)

[zin] = sin   (4)
[malz] = father   (5)
[kalt] = pen   (6)
[keltp] = rat   (7)

Answer : Studying the distribution of [d] and [z] from (1), (4); (3), (5), we can say that the mutual replacement of [d] and [z] do not affect the meaning of the words. [d] and [z] are in indentical environment too. So, [d] and [z] are not different phonemes, they are the allophones of the same phoneme in this particular language.

Problem-3 : Analyse the following data and say whether the [0] and [0 :] sounds are different phonemes or are the allophones of the same phoneme.

DATA

[li : t] = pen   (1)   [ikho :] = bed   (5)
[lit] = hen   (2)   [i : kho :] = bag (6)
[hetu :] = rat   (3)   [bino :] = tall   (7)
[hetu] = cat   (4)   [hinol] = short   (8)

Answer : Studying (1), (2) ; (3), (4) we can predict that the short vowels and the long vowels are in Contrastive Distribution. Their mutual replacement brings out the change in meaning of the words. On the basis of pattern study (Pattern Congruity) we may say that all short vowels of this language and their long counterparts are in Contrastive Distribution. So, [0] and [0 :] are two different phoneme. They cannot be the allophones of the same phoneme.

Problem-4 : Study the following data and say whether [p] and [t] are different phonemes or the allophones of the same phoneme in this language.

DATA

[pu : b] = student
[lpo : b] = he
[kpi ; t] = friend
[tmpi :] = she
[ntmpo :] = teacher
[pi : tn] = wonderful

Answer : Studying the above data we can say that [p] is always followed by long vowels (—long vowel). But [t] in this language occurs elsewhere. So, [p] and [t] are in complementary distribution. Let us examine whether they have sufficient phonetic similarity or not :

[p] = Bilabial **voiceless plosive**
[t] = Alveolar **voiceless plosive.**

For [p] and [t], they have two levels of similarities. So, [p] and [t] are the allophones of the same phoneme. They can not be different phonemes.

Structural Linguistics and Phonology 57

EXERCISES

1. What are the notions of Fardinand de Saussure?
2. What is the difference between *langue* & *parole* and 'Synchronic study' & 'Diachronic study?'
3. What is Phonology? What do you mean by 'minimal pair'?
4. What are the principles of phonemic analysis?
5. What is 'Pattern Congruity?' What do you mean by 'sufficient phonetic similarity?'
6. Solve the following problems :
   (i) Study the following data and say whether [m] and [n] are the different phonemes or the allophones of the same phoneme.

   [mpk] = rat   [nimpr] = brother
   [nlt] = fat   [lnpmt] = large
   [mkmt] = man   [pnpmk] = bag
   [bmtl] = run
   [bnbl] = dag
   [blni :]= love

   (ii) Analyse the following data and say whether [p] and [b] are the allophones of the same phoneme or not.

   [stepek] = branch
   [sel] = rat
   [stebek] = run
   [pa : tl] = fat
   [ba : di] = little
   [grb] = wife
   [ga : dle] = hat

[The data is from a Hypothetical language]

DEEP STRUCTURE & AMBIGUITY OF SENTENCES

In the 1957 model of Transformational Grammar, Noam Chomsky had the notion of a 'kernel' sentence. The Phrase Structure Rules (PSRs) generate the deep structure (underlying structure of sentences) strings for kernel sentences. Kernel sentences are of the following characteristics:
 (i) simple sentences, (ii) active sentences, (iii) declarative sentences, (iv) affirmative sentences.
 So, in Kernel sentence form passive sentences, interrogative sentences and negative sentences are omitted.

Deep Structure Phrase markers of Sentences
 1. The girl killed the boy.

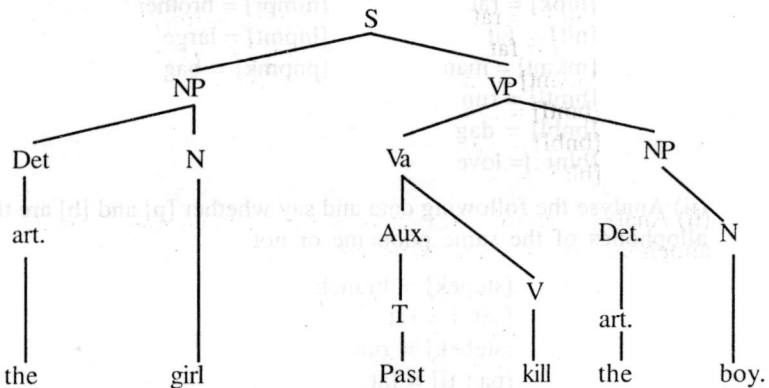

2. The boy was killed by the girl.
 The meaning of this sentence is same as (1)
 If the sentence is in passive voice, they make it active. Draw the deep Structure Tree.
 Active from = The girl killed the boy.

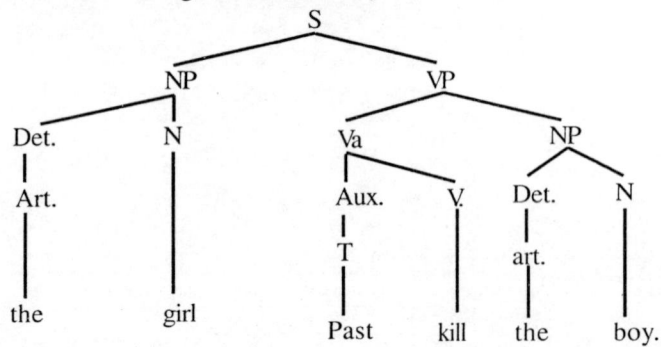

3. Birds I love.
   First, rewrite the sentence in the following form :
   I love birds.
   The tree diagram for this sentence is :

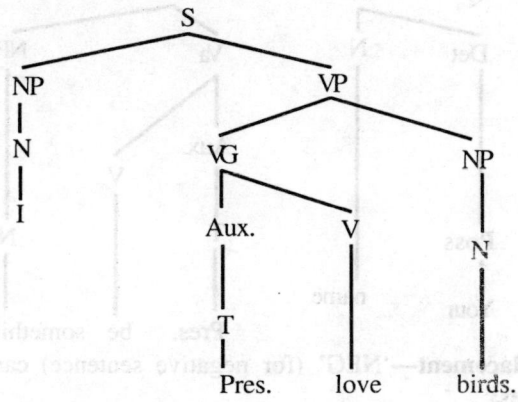

Interrogative Sentences:

4. Are you Swati?
   The tree diagram for this sentence is :

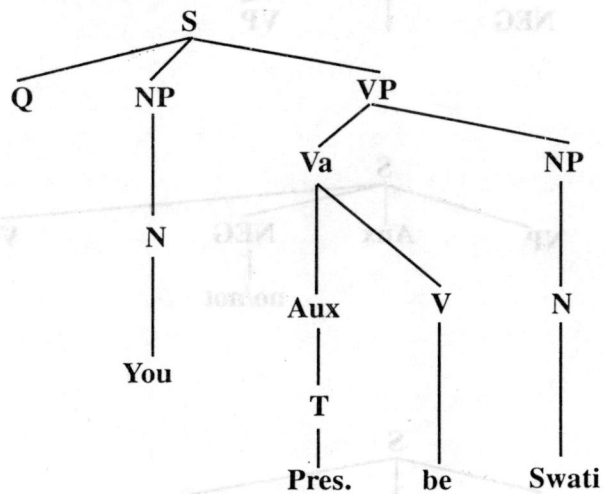

What is your name?
Actually, the sentence would be

$$\text{Your name is } \frac{\text{What}}{\text{(Something)}}$$

Now the tree diagram of the sentence can be drawn :

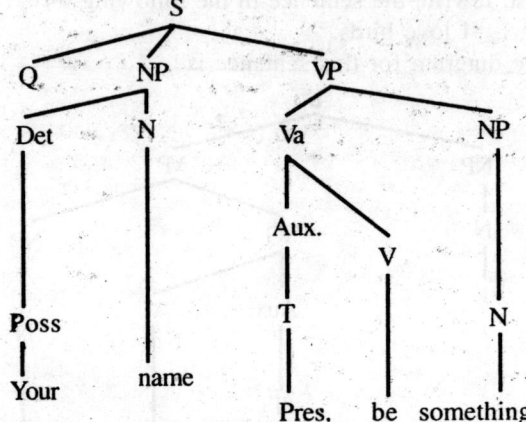

NEG Placement—'NEG' (for negative sentence) can be placed in different places:

5. (a)

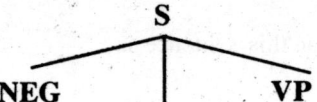

(b)

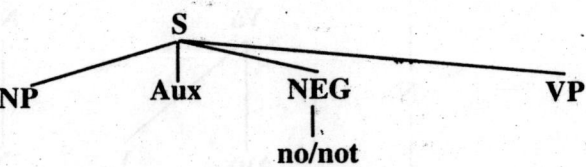

(c)

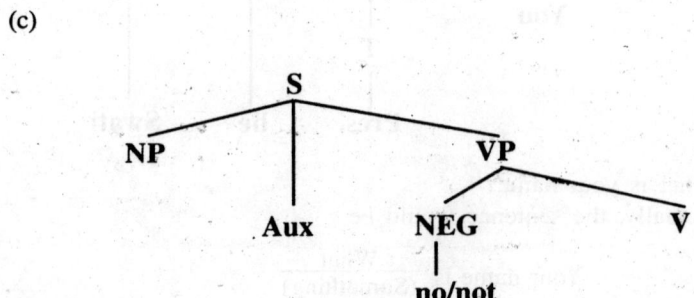

Deep Structure & Ambiguity of Sentences

For the simplicity of use we are to follow model (a) in our analysis of deep structures.

6. Sanjoy did not go.

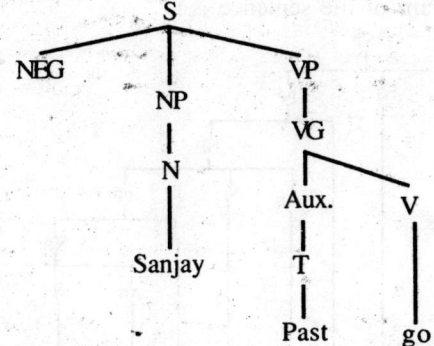

7. He was not playing cricket.

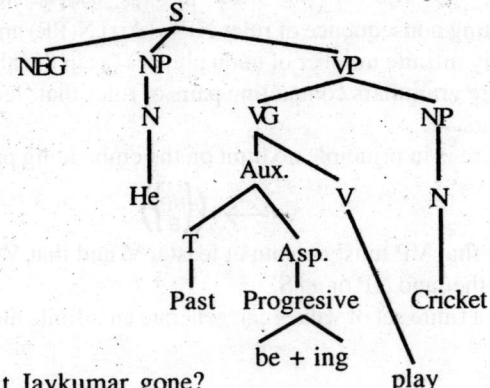

8. Why hasn't Jaykumar gone?

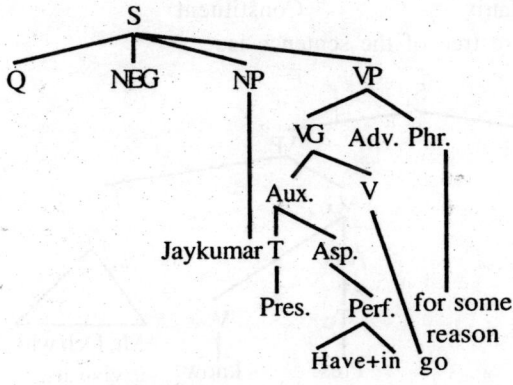

Embedding : The sentence that is embedded is called the constituent and the sentence into which it is embedded is called the matrix.
(9) The tiger is in the woods nearby the mountains.
The tree diagram of the sentence is :

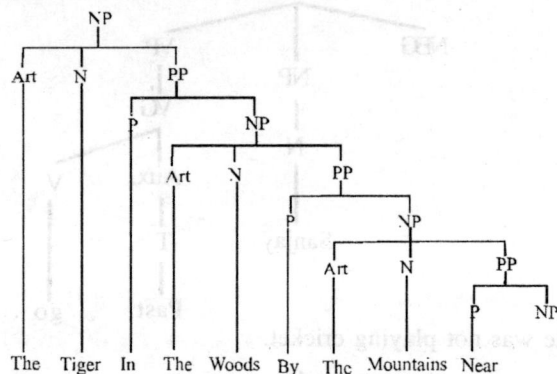

An interesting consequence of rules NP→(Art) N(PP) and PP—PNP generate a potentially infinite number of noun phrases (as in the above tree diagram). Phrase structure grammars containting pairs of rules that 'feed' one another are said to be recursive.
Indeed, there is in principle no limit on the embedding process.

$$VP \rightarrow V\left(\begin{Bmatrix} NP \\ S \end{Bmatrix}\right)$$

This states that VP must contain at least a V, and that V may optionally be followed by either and NP or an S.
Therefore, a finite set of values can generate an infinite number of sentences.

Example :
(10)   We know that Mr. Deb will visit us.
         Matrix   Constituent
Deep structure tree of the sentence is :

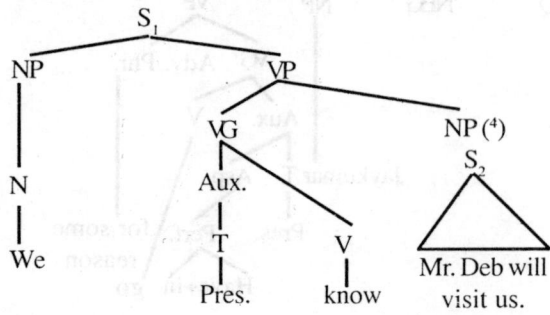

Deep Structure & Ambiguity of Sentences

(*) Mr. Deb will visit us (S_2)

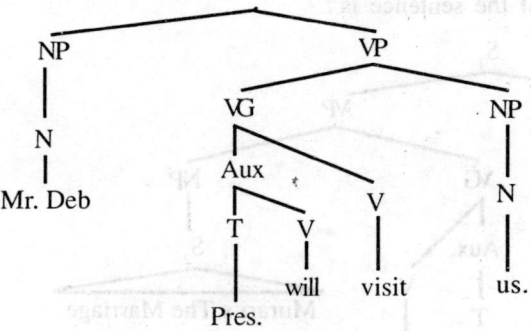

(11) That he is a good bowler is well known.
The tree diagram of the sentence is :

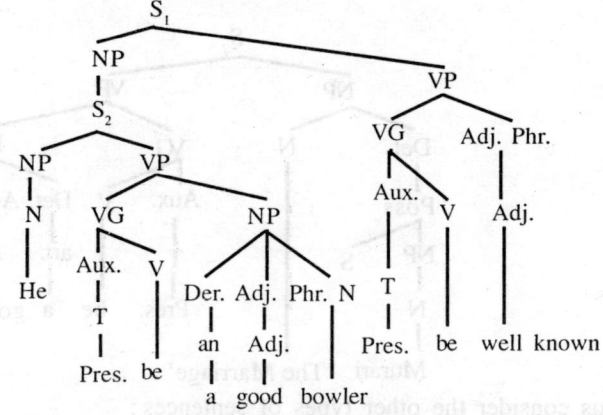

(12) The girl who is a researcher is beautiful.

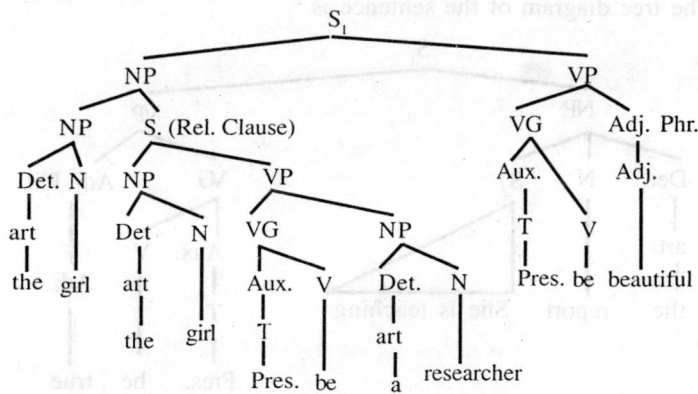

(13) He said that Murari's *The Marriage* is a good novel. The deep structure tree of the sentence is:

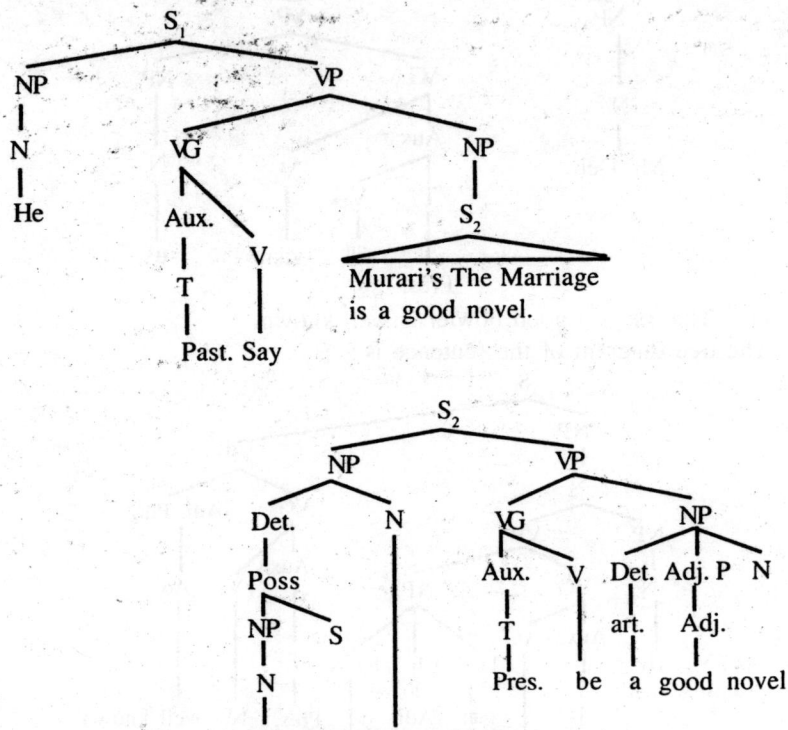

Let us consider the other types of sentences:
(14) The report that she is teaching is true.
The tree diagram of the sentence is:

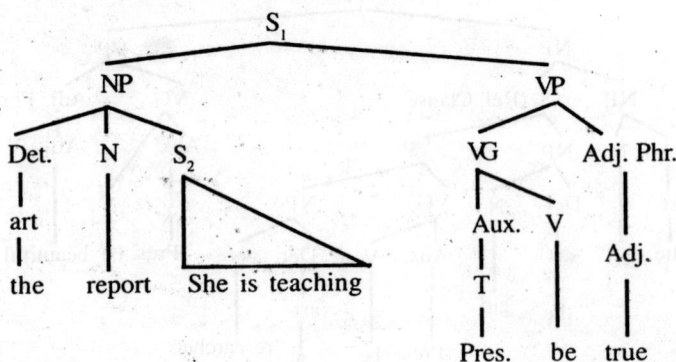

(15) To err is human.
Actually, we can consider the sentence:
Someone errs, is human.

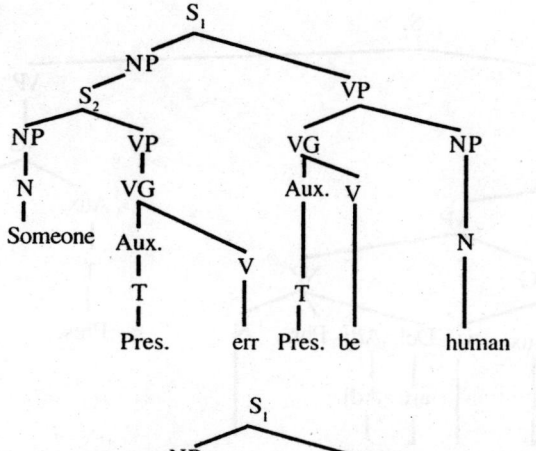

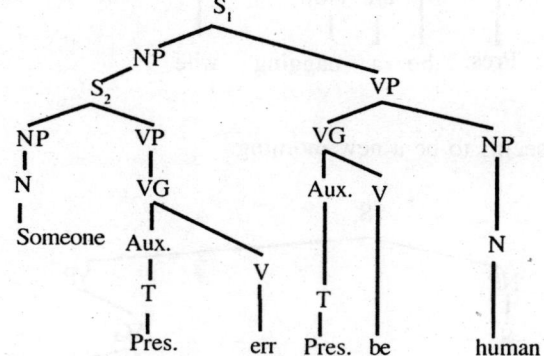

(16) To be or not to be is the question.
The tree diagram for the above sentence is:

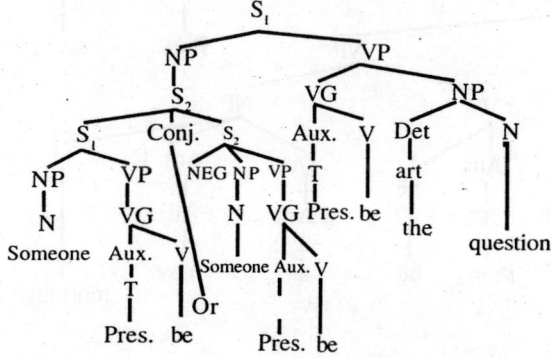

(17) She happens to be a nagging wife.
Verbs like, 'happen', 'seem', 'become' etc. are to be studied differently.
The tree diagram for the above sentence is :

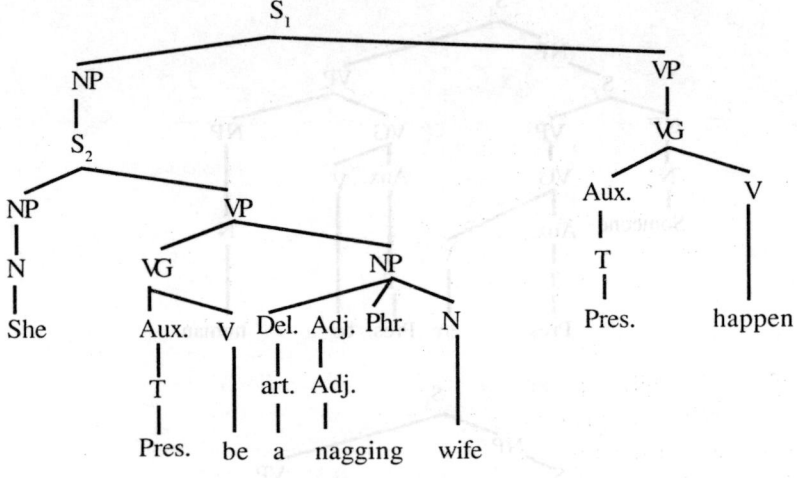

(18) It seems to be a new morning.

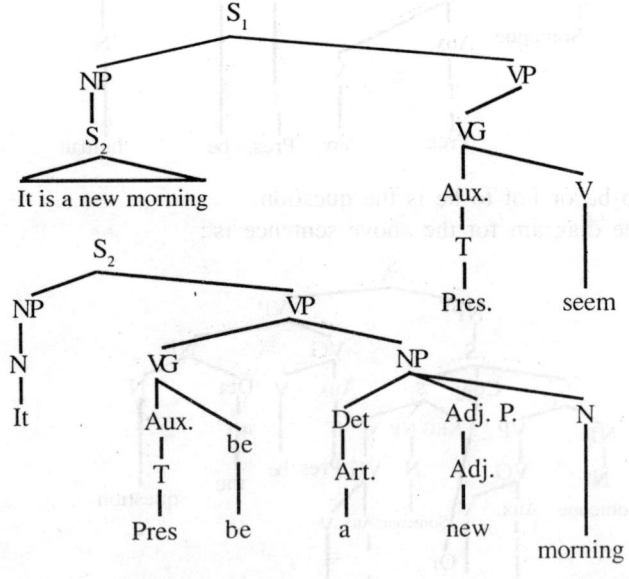

(19) Is it going to rain today?

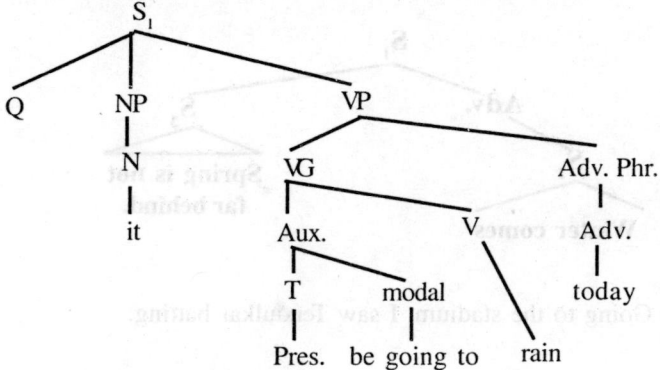

(20) He is too late to catch the train.

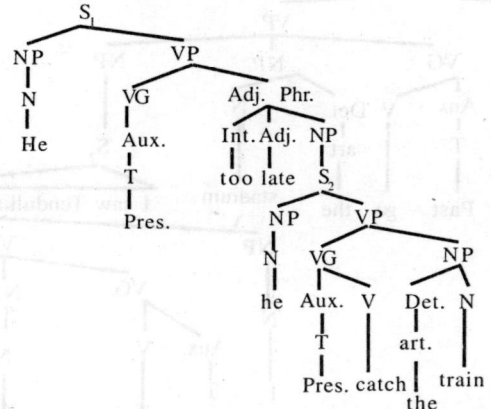

(21) Conditional clauses are responsible for a different diagram, Conditional sentences can be explained in $S_1 \rightarrow e$ Adv. S_2
If you come, I shall go.

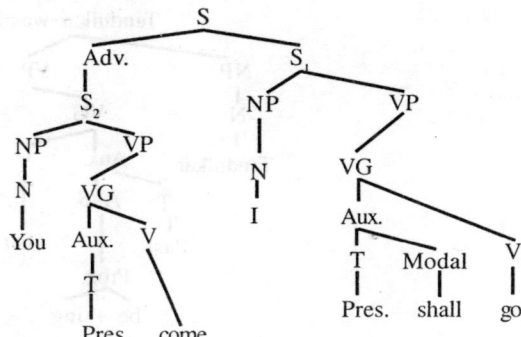

(22) If winter comes, spring is not far behind.

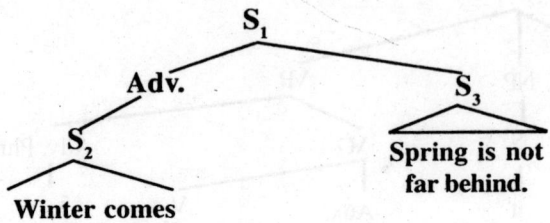

(23) Going to the stadium, I saw Tendulkar batting.

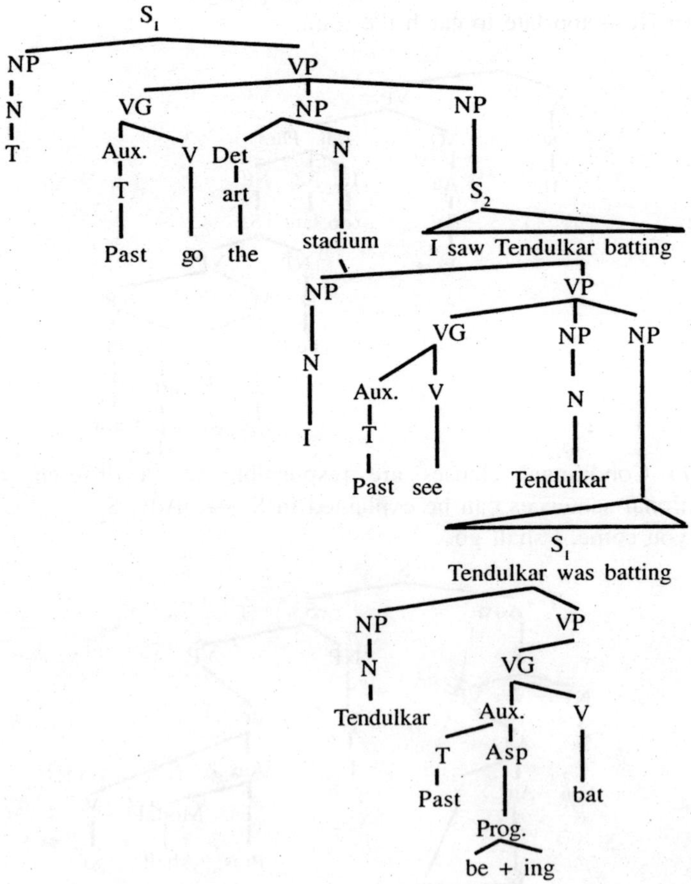

Deep Structure & Ambiguity of Sentences

(24) That the poet is writing the book is lazy.

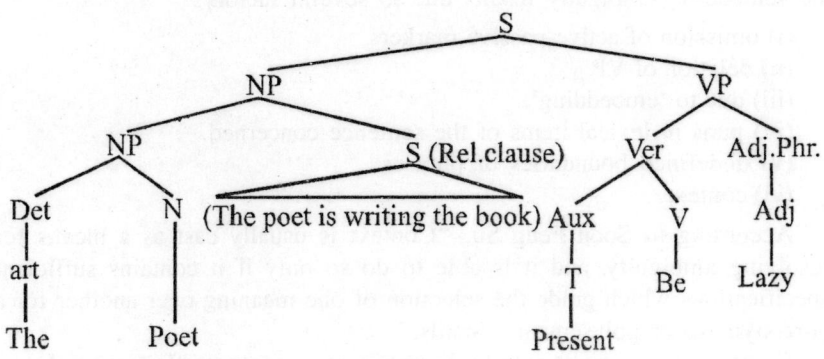

(25) That he is unprofessional is well-known.

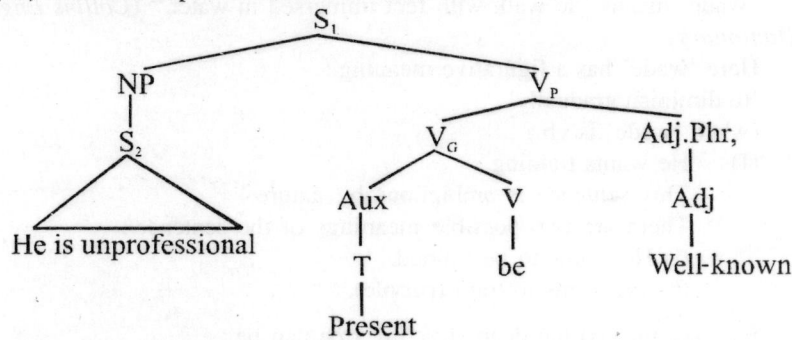

(26) She is intelligent but dishonest.

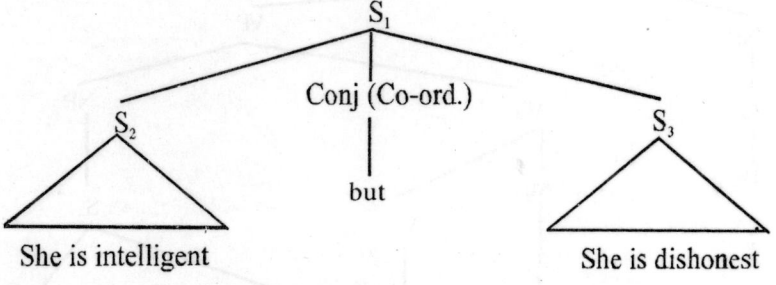

Ambiguity of Sentences : 'Ambiguity' means more than one meaning of the sentences. Ambiguity results due to several factors :

(i) omission of active-passive markers.
(ii) deletion of VP.
(iii) due to 'embedding'.
(iv) puns in lexical items of the sentence concerned.
(v) undefined boundaries of phrases.
(vi) context.

According to Soon Peng Su, "Context is usually cast as a means for resolving ambiguity, and it is able to do so only if it contains sufficient specifications which guide the selection of one meaning over another for a homonymous or polysemantic words."

Context plays a great role to disambiguate a sentence. For example, (from Hopkings *The Lantern Out of Door*.)

'Wade' means "to walk with feet immersed in water." (*Collins English Dictionary*)

Here 'wade' has a figurative meaning :
'to diminish gradually'
(when 'wade' is vb.)

(1)   He wants training.
      This sentence is ambiguous by nature.
      There are two possible meanings of the sentence :
      (i) He wants to be trained.
      (ii) He wants to train (people).

For meaning (i) the deep structure tree can be :

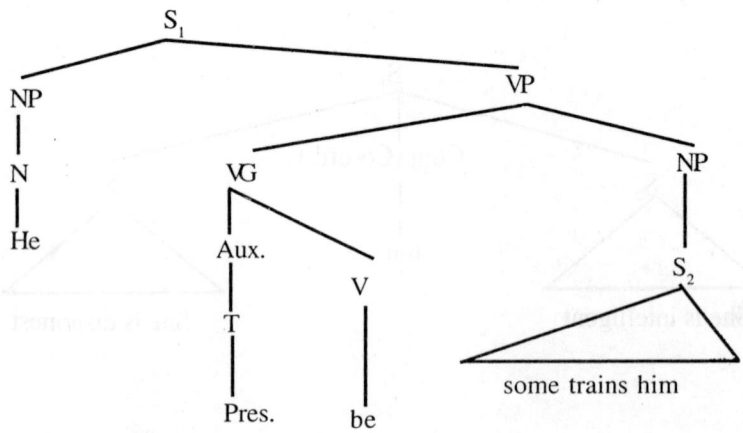

For meaning (ii) the tree diagram is :

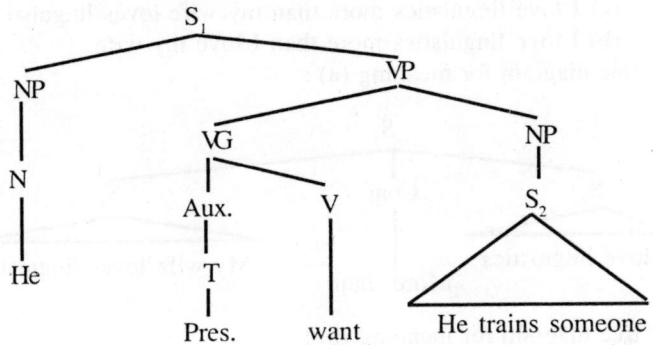

(2) I love Indian poetry and novels.

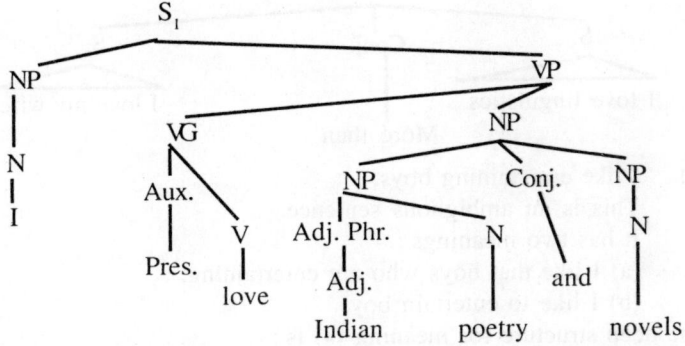

The above diagram stands for—I love Indian poetry and novels (not Indian)—M_1

But the sentence has another meaning :
I love Indian poetry and Indian novels. —M_2
For M_2, the NP is shown below :

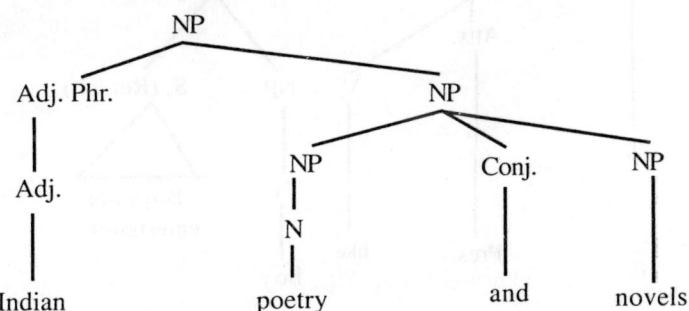

(3) I love Linguistics more than my wife.
This sentence has two meanings :
(a) I love linguistics more than my wife loves linguistics.
(b) I love linguistics more than I love my wife.
The tree diagram for meaning (a) :

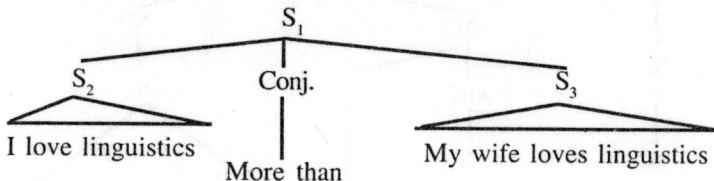

The tree diagram for meaning (b) :

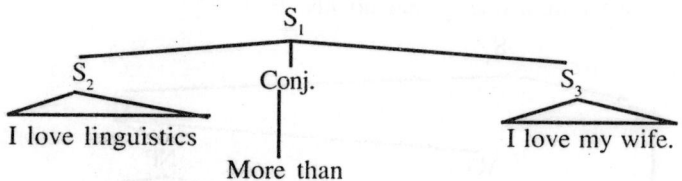

(4) I like entertaining boys.
This is an ambiguous sentence.
It has two meanings :
(a) I like that boys who are entertaining.
(b) I like to entertain boys.
The deep structure for meaning (a) is :

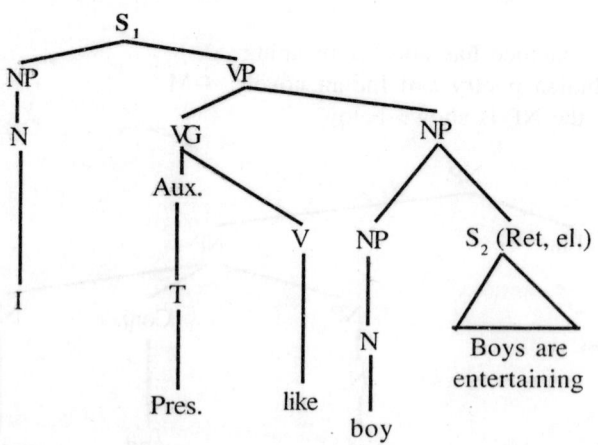

The tree diagram for meaning (b) is :

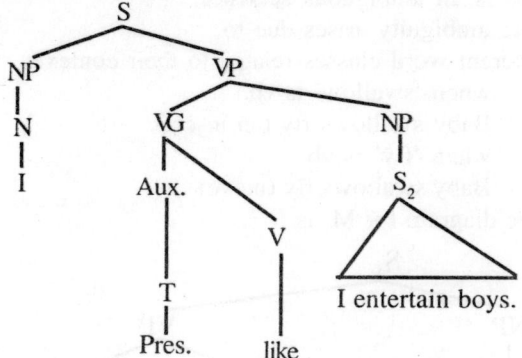

(5) John left her unhappy.
The above sentence is ambiguous by nature.
It has two meanings :
M_1—John left here... she was unhappy.
M_2—John left her... he (John) was unhappy.

For M_1 the tree diagram is :

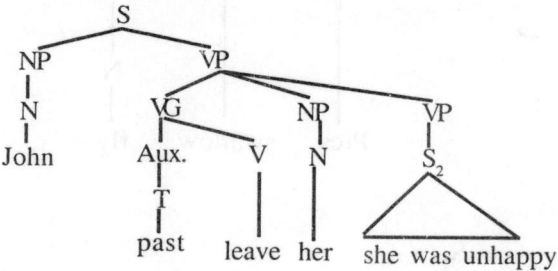

For M_2 :

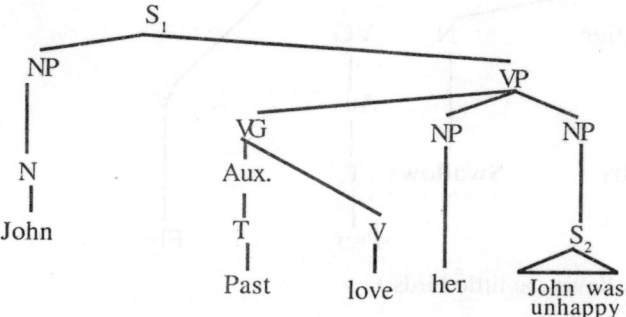

(6) Baby swallows fly.
    This is an ambiguous sentence.
    Here ambiguity arises due to
    different word classes related to their contexts.
    M_1 when 'swallow' is vb.
         Baby swallows fly (an insect).
    M_2 when 'fly' is vb.
         Baby swallows fly (move)
The tree diagram for M_1 is :

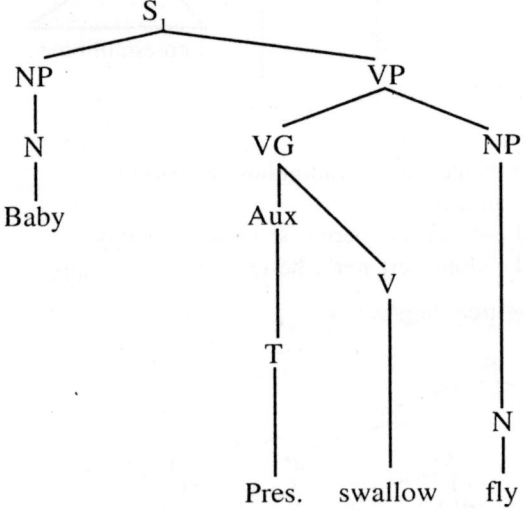

For M_2

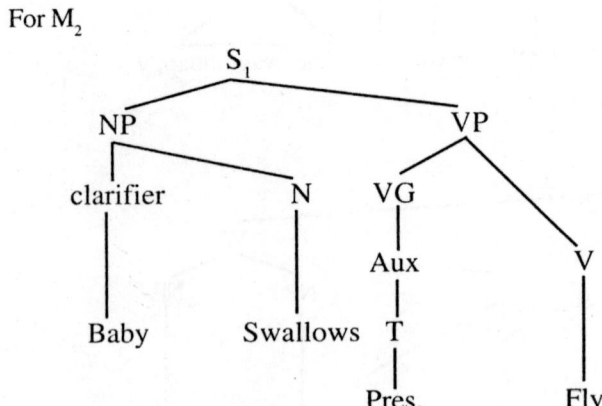

(Here, swallows are little birds.)

Deep Structure & Ambignity of Sentences

(7) The mother of the boy and girl will arrive soon.
—This sentence is ambiguous; that is, it has more than one meaning. It is a case of structural ambiguity. It is either about one person (the mother) or about two persons (the mother and the girl).

For meaning (1)

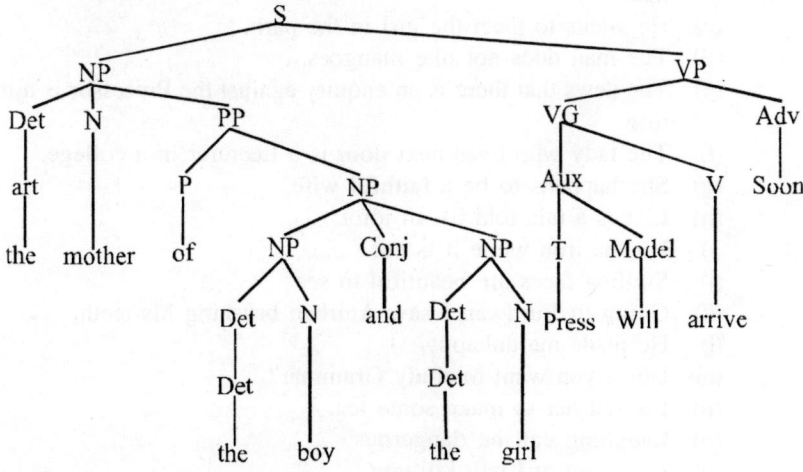

For meaning (2):

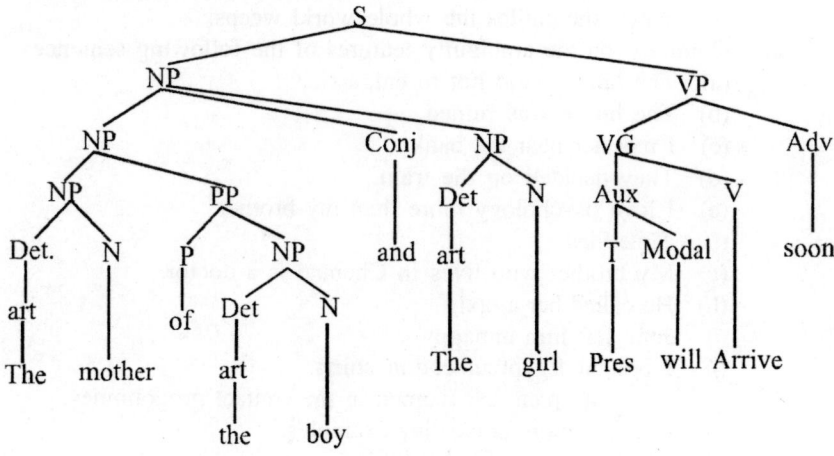

EXERCISES

1. Draw deep structure phrase markers of the following sentences :—
   (a) The minister was hackled by the people.
   (b) The social workers were given a lot of money by a business man.
   (c) He wants to meet the girl in the park.
   (d) The man does not like mangoes.
   (e) The news that there is an enquiry against the Professor is not true.
   (f) The lady who lives next door is a Lecturer in a college.
   (g) She happens to be a faithful wife.
   (h) Life is a tale told by an idiot.
   (i) Hit the iron while it is hot.
   (j) Smiling faces are beautiful to see.
   (k) Going to Burdwan I saw Anirban brushing his teeth.
   (l) He made me unhappy.
   (m) Don't you want to study Grammar?
   (n) I asked her to make some tea.
   (o) Laughing can be dangerous.
   (p) Drop that or I will kill you.
   (q) The teacher is one who teaches.
   (r) God seems to be dishonest.
   (s) When she smiles the whole world weeps.

2. Commeat on the ambiguity features of the following sentences.
   (a) The lamb is too hot to eat.
   (b) The house was ruined.
   (c) I met her near the bank.
   (d) They decided on the train.
   (e) I love psychology more than my brother.
   (f) Time flies.
   (g) My brother who lives in Chennai is a doctor.
   (h) He called her a taxi.
   (i) John left him unhappy.
   (j) I bought Egyptian cotton shirts.
   (k) I met old men and women in the contact programmes.
   (l) Give me more interesting examples.
   (m) We are not teaching-machines.

Differences of Sentences

The sentences can differ both in respect of structure and meaning. Let us take the sentences :
(a) The bus is stopping. (b) The bus stops.

These two sentences are different both in respect of structure and meaning. The meaning of sentence (a) is—the bus is stopping (in a particular point of time). This sentence carries the Present Continuous Tense. In sentence (b), the meaning is—The bus stops (habit). This sentence carries the simple Present Tense to denote present habit.

The structure (tree diagram) for sentence (a) :

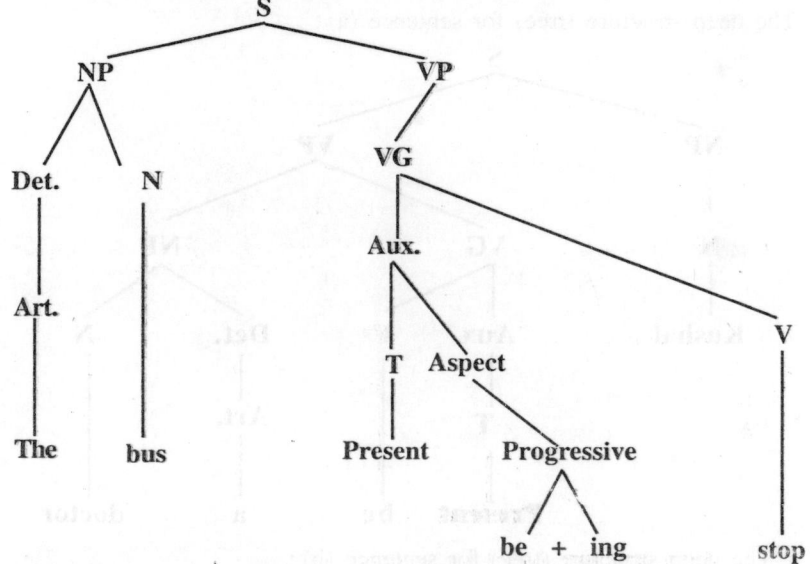

The structure (tree diagram) for sentence (b) :

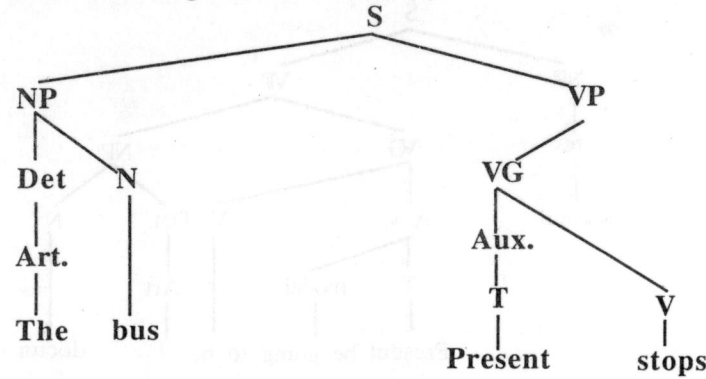

Now, let us examine another pair of sentences :
(a) Kushal is a doctor.
(b) Kushal is going to be a doctor.

Sentence (a) means Kushal has become a doctor whereas sentence (b) means Kushal will be a doctor in future. In sentence (a), the fact is a reality (present), but in sentence (b), the fact is a future possibility. So these two sentences differ in respect of meaning.

Sentence (a) & sentence (b) are different in respect of structure too. The difference lies at the level of VG. Sentence (b) carries a modal 'be going to' which refers the 'possible world' (future possibility). Sentence (a) is a simple fact,. Here VG carries only Tense & Verb items.

The deep structure (tree) for sentence (a) :

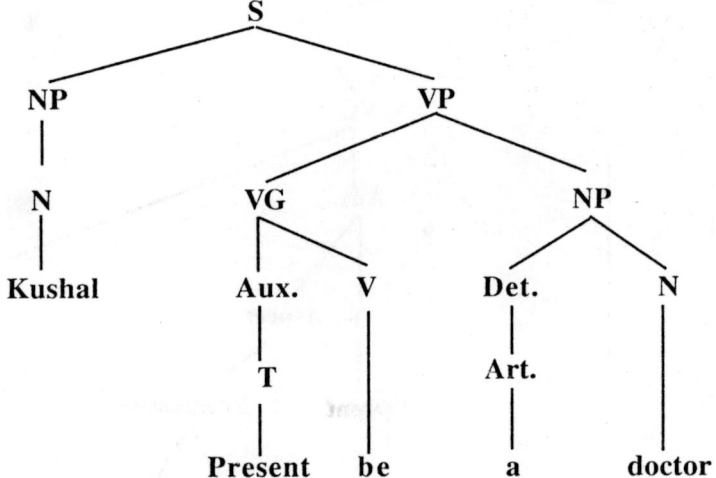

The deep structure (tree) for sentence (b) :

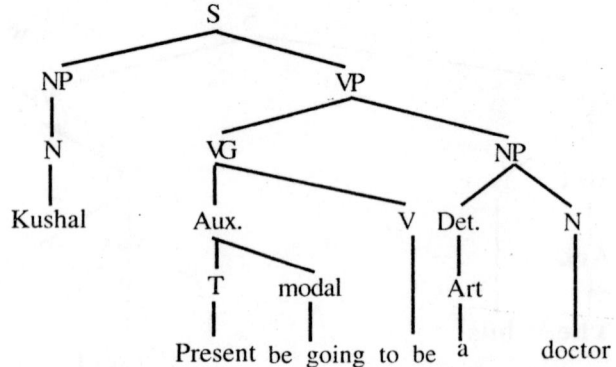

EXERCISES

Comment on the difference of the following pairs of sentences :
- (i) (a) It worked loosely.
    - (b) It worked loose.
- (ii) (a) John is eager to please.
    - (b) John is easy to please.
- (iii) (a) Aniruddha is expected to reach here by two o'clock.
    - (b) Aniruddha will reach here by two o'clock.
- (iv) (a) He felt nothing.
    - (b) He felt exhausted.
- (v) (a) He has been living in Guntur for two years.
    - (b) He has been living in Guntur since 1985.
- (vi) (a) He is going to marry in November.
    - (b) He is getting married in November.
- (vii) (a) I have become a national cricketer.
    - (b) I am going to be a national cricketer.
- (viii) (a) My book on ELT will be released soon.
    - (b) My book on ELT has been released.
- (ix) (a) You need to be honest.
    - (b) You are honest.
- (x) (a) I had to follow the rules of income tax.
    - (b) I followed the rules of income tax.
- (xi) (a) Roon is likely to be a teacher.
    - (b) Roon becomes a teacher.
- (xii) (a) Bin would like to attend the meeting.
    - (b) Bin attends the meeting.

ARTICLE FEATURES

Articles are a small sub-set. They come under determiners (det.). Traditionally, 'the' refers to definiteness and 'a' and 'an' refer to indefinitenes of the references of an NP (Noun Phrase). But, articles do not behave accordingly. For example, "The child is the father of Man."

In the above example 'the' refers to a class. So, the reference is not definite but 'generic' by character.

(A) *Generic References :*
    (a) With indefinite articles—
Examples, (i) *An* elephant is a big animal. (ii) A lion is a kind-hearted animal.
    (b) With definite articles—
Examples :
      (i) *The* Indians are known for their culture.
      (ii) *The* rich have their richness to share.
    (c) **Zero** article—
      (i) He likes (**Zero**) tea.
      (ii) (**Zero**) teachers are to take classes at different places.

If the reference is Generic we must say as + GEN.

(B) *Specific Reference :*
    (a) With Definite article—
Examples :
He bought a pen but he later returned *the* pen to the shop.
Here 'the' is —GEN
    + Specific
    (Anaphoric reference)
    (b) With Indefinite article—
Example : I want to meet *a* girl.
Here the article is—GEN
    + Specific

In specific references we may not identify the person/thing with which the article is attached with.

    (c) Definite Reference :
The Endocrine specialist cured the girl.

Here, in this specific context listener can easily identify the endocrine specialist.

So, the reference is definite.

We can now say the reference is

$$\begin{bmatrix} -\text{Gen} \\ +\text{Specific} \\ +\text{Definite} \end{bmatrix}$$

Article Features

In this reference the listener can easily identify (the reference) the person/thing.

If the reference is +Definite, we must find out whether the reference is Situational or Linguistic.

The clue to the identification of the definiteness of the reference may be arrived at through situation. Situational references can be of two types :
    (a) immediate.
    (b) general.

Example of the Immediate situational reference—Go to *the* door.

Example of the General situational reference—*The* sun sets in the west.

The Linguistic clue may help the listener to identify the definiteness of the reference. Linguistic references can be Anaphoric & Cataphoric.

Anaphoric reference—

He is *a reputed doctor.*

I want to meet *a doctor.*

Here, 'a doctor' refers to 'a reputed doctor', mentioned earlier.

Cataphoric reference—Here the linguistic clue occurs after the head Noun of the NP.

Example :
The lady who went to Santiniketan is my wife.

Here, the head noun is 'lady'. The clue is 'who went to Santiniketan'. The definiteness arises out of the set. clause structure of the sentence. So the reference of the above sentence (the article feature of *'the* lady') is :

$$\begin{bmatrix} -\text{Gen} \\ +\text{Specific} \\ +\text{Definite} \end{bmatrix}$$

(linguistic reference,
the reference is Cataphoric)

We can put the whole chart in the following way :

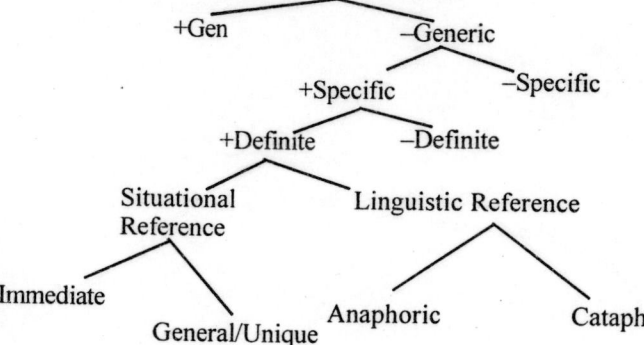

Now, let us examine the article features of 'the' in the following sentence : Tendulkar is called *the* Bradman of Indian cricket.

$$\begin{bmatrix} -\text{Gen} \\ +\text{Specific} \\ +\text{Definite} \\ \text{Situational Reference.} \end{bmatrix}$$

The Reference is Unique/General because everyone can identify the situational reference.

EXERCISES

1. Examine the articles features of the underlined NPs in the following expressions.
   (a) During *the Ramzan* of the year.
   (b) *The Sun* rises in the East.
   (c) I love *the man*, who writes stories of adventure.
   (d) Dr. Maji is *a famous doctor*.
   (e) *A man* wants to meet him.
   (f) *The poor* have no friends in the locality.
   (g) I want *the pen*, which is on the table.
   (h) *The girl* I saw near Tarnaka was ill.
   (i) Give the baby *some milk* please.
   (j) Rajat wants to buy *a novel* written by Dr. Dhamija.

PHRASE STRUCTURE RULES
MODERN THEORIES OF LINGUISTICS

Phrase Structure Rules are the rewriting rules. A single arrow sign is used to refer to the Phrase Structure Rules (PSRs). PSRs are used to generate the deep structure (under-lying structure) strings. For example: "Character is Destiny" is a sentence. And the PSRs are the following :

PSR 1. S → NP VP
PSR 2. NP → N
PSR 3. N → Character, destiny
PSR 4. VP → VG NP
PSR 5. VG → Aux.
PSR 6. Aux → Tense (T)
PSR 7. V → be

These PSRs are applied to get the deep structure phrase marker (in the form of tree diagram in the following way :

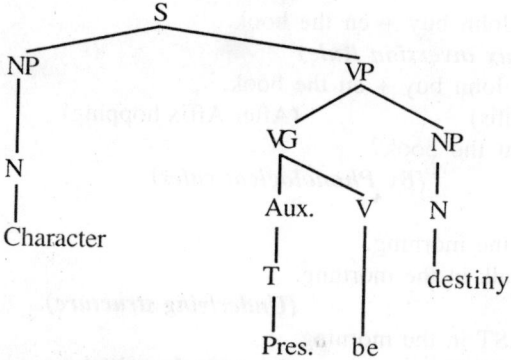

The Chomsky Revolution

Chomsky made a crusade against the Structural Linguistics. He challenged the age-old rules of the American Structuralism.

(i) For Chomsky, language is not habit or behaviour. Language is creative and innate by nature. For Chomsky, language is not only 'parole' but also 'langue'. Chomsky was influenced by the cognitive school. Chomsky differed with the Structuralists on the basic proposition regarding language.

(ii) Noam Chomsky also discarded the objective of linguistic analysis. For him, the objective of linguistic analysis is to construct an expirical theory of language.

(iii) Chomsky also challenged the notion of 'linguistic corpus' as the data for language study. By language, Chomsky meant 'linguistic competence'.

(iv) Chomsky challenged the notion of 'discovery procedure' of the Structuralists. He proposed an alternative model—. Evaluation Procedure'. This procedure evaluates which grammar is the better grammar in the concerned language.

Chomsky proposes a new model for language—TG (Transformational Grammar). Chomsky calls his model Transformational Generative Grammar. 'Generative' the very term for Chomsky, means to 'explain' (not 'produce'). Generative Grammar explains all the (possible) sentences in a language. Chomsky also talks about 'weak generative capacity' and 'strong generative capacity' of grammar to generate the sentences of a particular language. Generative Grammar makes use of T-Rules (Transformational Rules) to derive to surface structure from the deep structure. So, TRs act exactly the opposite way of PSRs.

Application of T-Rules
Example—(i)
'Has John bought the book?" The underlying structure of this sentence is :
[John] Present have—en buy the book.
NP
Present + have John buy + en the book.
(After Subj.—Aux inversion Rule)
Have + Present John buy + en the book.
(Vbl)   (Affix)   (After Affix hopping)
Has John bought the book?
                 (By Phonological rules)
Example—(ii)
John walked in the morning.
John PAST + walk in the morning.
                         (Underlying structure)
John walk + PAST in the morning.
    (Vbl)   (Affix)   *(by Affix hopping)*
John walked in the morning.
                         (by Phonological rules)

Example—(iii)
Is Mary singing in the room?
[Mary] PRESENT be-ing sing in the room.
NP   *(Underlying structure)*
PRESENT + by Mary ing + Sing in the room.
                         (sub.—Aux. inversion Rule)
be + PRESENT Mary sing + ing in the room.
                         (by Affix Hopping)
Is Mary singing in the room?
                         (by Phonological rules)

Phrase Structure Rules 85

Affix hopping—This is also known as affix switch. The process of Affix hopping can be shown in the following way :

Affix	Verbal items	
A	B	⇒ B + A
PAST	Will	Will + PAST
–EN	have	Have + EN
–ING	be	Be + ING

Actually, Affix—Vbl ⇒ 2 + 1
             1   2

Wh-Movement Rule—This is also an important T-Rule. The Wh-word is introduced before the S–HV Inversion rule is applied for this purpose. For all direct questions inversion (Wh-fronting) is obligatory.
Example :
What is your name?
Your name is what.
            (Underlying Structure)

What you name is. (wh-fronting)
What is your name? (Aux. inversion)

Topicalization : It is a process by which certain types of constituents in a sentence can be moved to the front of the sentence to form the TOPIC of the sentence. The TOPIC means 'Theme' of the sentence. It is a focusing rule to form the TOPIC of a sentence.
Example :
I likes **fishes**.
       TOPIC
Fishes I like.
(TOPIC)

Deletion—
(a) **Deletion of Subject—**
    (i)   GO home.
    (ii) Shut up!
    ('You' is deleted)
(b) **Deletion of Wh-words in relative clauses—**
    (i)   The man (Whom) we saw...
    (ii) The jatra (Which/that) I saw...
(c) **Deletion of VP—**
    (i)   Nirmal went to Kolkata, and Abhijit (went) to Sagar.
    (ii) Indranil talked to Joyjit, and Sudev (talked) to Parijat.
(d) **Deletion of identical element—**
    (i)   Mitra is as tall as I am (tall).
    (ii) Mr. Verma is as good as Mr. Rao is (good).

Some Modern Theories of Linguistics

(a) Government-Building (GB) Theory—It is also known as 'Principles and Parameters' approach. This approach assumes that Universal Grammar includes some fixed principles and some 'not closed' (open) parameters. This approach uses : (i) The projection principle. (ii) The (*Theta*) Criterion and (iii) "Null Subject Parameter."

The Empty Category Principle (ECP) assumes that if a category (place) is empty, then it should be 'governed' properly. Therefore, this method is known as 'Government-Binding' (GB).

The Binding theory assumes the conditions under which Noun Phrases (NPs) are interpreted as Co-referential with other NPs in the same existing sentence.

To meet the purpose, NPs are classified into the following heads:

(a) Anaphors (reflexive and reciprocal pronouns in English)

(b) Pronominals (NPs which lack lexical content).

(c) Referential Expressions (NPs with definite lexical content)

(b) Sysmatic Functional Grammar (SFG)—This model has roots in Halliday. This model talks about ideational, interpersonal and textual functions of language. It is a Neo-Firthian concept of language. This model is based on the functional aspect of language.

(c) Case Grammar—According to Fillmore, Case Grammar is a "substantive modification to the theory of transformational grammar." Fillmore prepares a list of the case categories:

(i) Agentive (A)
(ii) Dative (D)
(iii) Factitive (F)
(iv) Instrumental (I)
(v) Locative (L)
(vi) Objective (O)
(vii) Benefactive (B)
(viii) Comitative (C)

In grammar, verbs which are in the deep structure can be selected according to "the case environment the sentence provides".

For example, the verbs like "open" & "remove" can take an AGENT and an OBJECT.

So, for 'open' and 'remove' the case frame can be :

[– O + A]

Examples,   [– O] The window opened.

[– O + A] Rajib opened the window.

The case categories are represented by NPs working in case relationships with the verb.

X-bar Theory—X is a category variable in X-bar theory. X is used in the conventional categories of noun, verb, adj., adv., etc. There are intermediate stages in the formation of phrases. We can start with NP level.

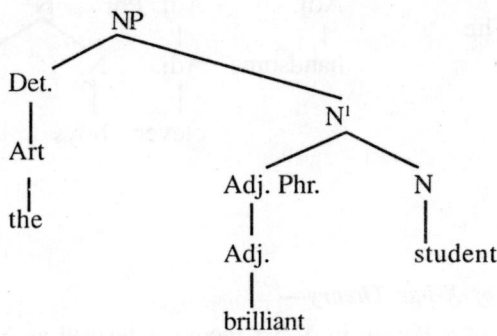

[N^1 = Noun bar]

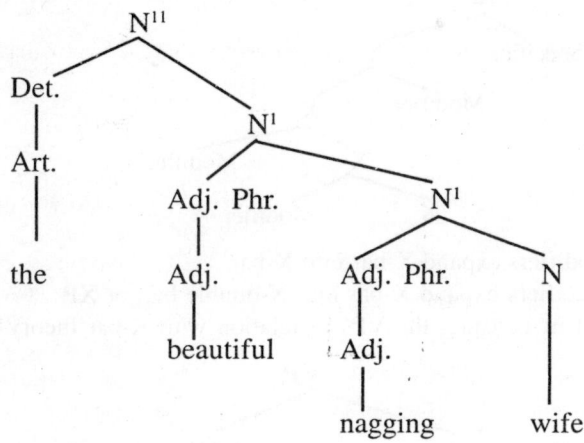

[N^{11} = Noun double bar]
In the second NP, 'beautiful nagging wife' is an intermediate sequence.
The complements are with a close relationship with the head of the phrases. For example :

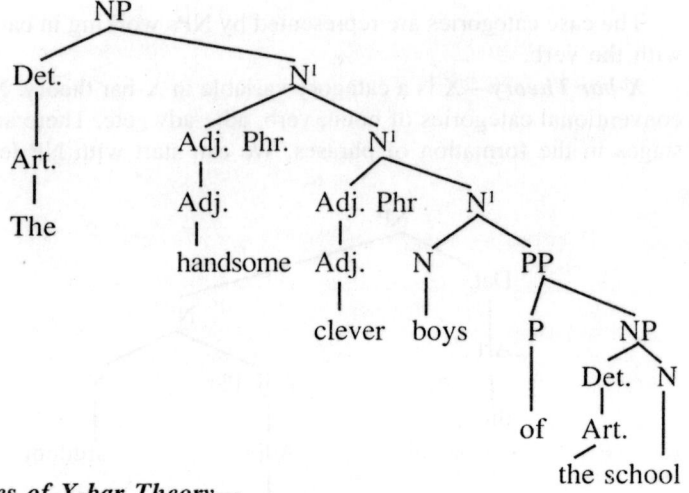

Some Rules of X-bar Theory—

(i) The head of a Phrase in X-bar theory is termed as X. X stands for Nouns, Verb, Adj, and so on.
(ii) Complements expand X into X-bar.

For example :

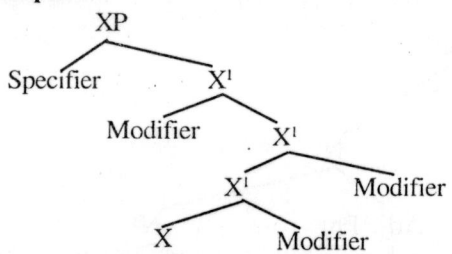

(iii) Modifiers expand X-bar into X-bar.
(iv) Specifiers expand X-bar into X-double bar, or XP.
Now let us consider the VPs in relation with X-bar theory—

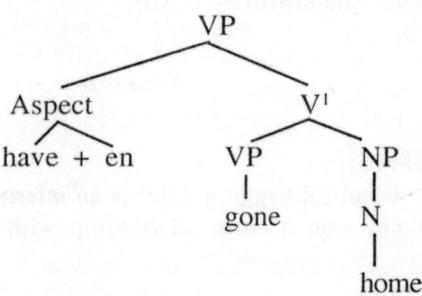

Sentences can be analysed in terms of X-bar theory. I is the head of inflectional Phrases' (IP).

Example:

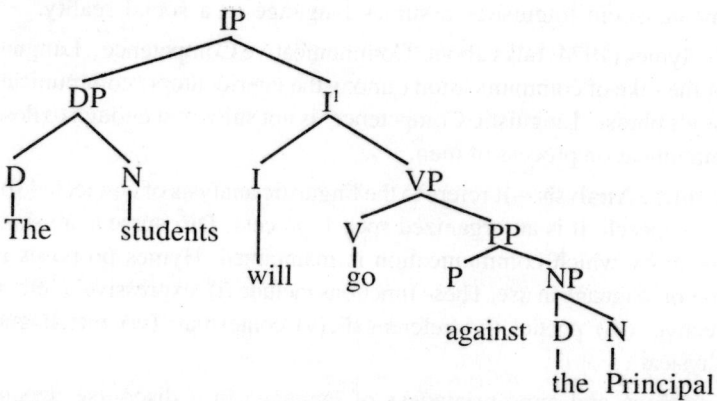

The above sentence is the projection of the modal auxiliary 'will' ; which is realised to I¹ by a complement VP 'go against the Principal' and to IP by a specifier 'the students'. Now X-bar theory has become a standard modal of syntactical analysis.

(e) Componential Theory—Componential theory proposes a set of componential for lexical items. Americal anthropologists devised this method in 1950. In this theory the individual items are decomposed into 'semantic primes' with only (+) sets.

For Example :

Bachelor—[+ male] [+ adult] [+ human]
            [+ unmarried]
Wife—[+ female] [+ adult] [+ married]
        [+ human]

This theory makes use of semantic markers, distinguishers, and many other related aspects to arrive at a universal inventory of semantic features, which are present in the language.

SOCIAL ASPECTS OF LANGUAGE

Language is an artefact of society. Language represents the whole fabric of the socio-cultural life of people. It is individual as well as social phenomena. Socio linguistics assumes language as a social reality.

Dell Hymes (1974) talks about 'Communicative Competence'. Language is used for the sake of communication (among the interlocutors / communicators). Chomsky's phrase 'Linguistic Competence' is not sufficient enough to describe the communication process of men.

Discourse Analysis—It refers to the linguistic analysis of connected spoken or written speech. It is an organized speech process. Discourse analysis is the mechanism by which communication is maintained. Hymes proposes seven functions of language in use. These functions include (i) 'expressive' / 'emotive', (ii) 'directive', (iii) 'poetic', (iv) 'referential', (v) 'contextual', (vi) 'metalinguistic', (vii) 'physical'.

Acceptance and appropriateness of language in a discourse depend on several factors. The factors which go into the process of discourse are mentioned below :

    (i) addresser (sender)
    (ii) addressee (receiver)
    (iii) topic of discourse
    (iv) code (linguistic)
    (v) Channel (speech or writing)
    (vi) situation or context.

Discourse Analysis uses 'Speech Act', and 'Speech situation' rules.

A speech situation includes the factors related to :

(a) contexts, (b) objectives, (c) addresser & addressee

Speech acts can be divided into three heads : (i) Locutionary Acts. (ii) Illocutionary Acts. (iii) Perlocutionary Acts.

Socio-pragmatics, which is a recent development to study 'discourse', proposes interactive styles for communication. The 'Conceptual Dependences Representation' (CD Representation) is a modern model to analyse discourse. This model studies the message of discourse (including 'off-topic acts') in relation with language.'

Acceptability of Sentences : Acceptability of sentences depends on linguistic factors as well as on social issues. Sentences on the basis of acceptability and unacceptability can be represented in the following diagram.

Social Aspects of Language

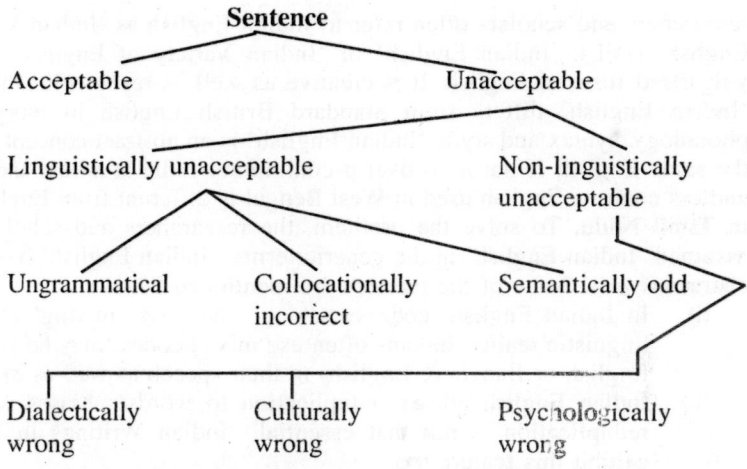

Examples of unacceptable sentences :

1. I have been teaching in a Govt. school *since* five years.
   (Grammatically wrong)
2. I prefer *feble* tea. (Collocationally incorrect)
3. *In* accident we met in Hyderabad.
   (Collocationally incorrect)
4. The river *loves* the house. (Semantically wrong)
5. I shall *return back*.
   I met *Anu Auntie*.
6. I met kumar at the Nampalli Statio. The weather was good. We sat together. But he was *grass* to me.
   ['grass' means inferior
   This is typically a slant usage] (Socially incorrect)
7. She was disturbed by her past. She started journing down the memory lane. *She eats rice. She is a faithful wife of Mr. Guha.*
   (Psychologically wrong)
   —Here the thoughts are fragmentary by nature. They are not planned in an order.

Indian English—English has been 'x-ised' ('x' can be India, Srilanka, Australia....) through the process of socio-cultural as well as socio-linguistic acculturation. In India, English co-exists in a 'diglossic' relationship with regional languages like Tamil, Bangla, Marathi, Assamese, etc. In a culturally and linguistically pluralistic Indian subcontinent English is used as the 'Second Language' (L_2). Indian English is socio-linguistic reality today. We need a broadbased survey to say whether Indian English is a 'Pidgin' or not. But, it is a fact that English has been nativised in Indian context. Some researchers and scholars often refer to Indian English as 'Indian Variety of English' (IVE). 'Indian English' or 'Indian Variety of English' is not a vulgarised form of English. It is creative as well as resourceful by nature. 'Indian English' differs from Standard British English in morphology, phonology, syntax and style. 'Indian English' is an abstract concept because the same English is not used over a continuum. India is a vast and almost endless country. English used in West Bengal is different from English used in Tamil Nadu. To solve the problem, the researchers and scholars have assumed 'Indian English' in the generic terms. 'Indian English' has several characteristics. Some of the features are mentioned below :

(i) In Indian English 'code switching' and 'code mixing' are socio-linguistic reality. Indians often use mixed codes (may be Hindi and English or Bangla & English) in their speech as well as in writing.

(ii) Indian English allows reduplication to words/ phrases when the reduplication is not that essential. 'Indian Writings in English' exhibit this feature too.

(iii) In Indian English hybrids (Indian words & Indian affixes/ inflections) are used frequently.

Example :

lathi	+	*charged*
Indian word		Eng. word
	=	lathi charged (hybrid)
gharao	+	*ed* = *gharaoed*
(Indian word)		(inflection (hybrid) of Eng.)

In Indian English sometimes Present Continuous Tense is used in place of Present Perfect Continuous Tense.

For example :

I am living in Howrah for two years.

(v) Many Indian words are passed into Indian English register. For example, coolie, sahib, dada, ma-bap, deshi, golkamra, Kumkum mark, Munsi, atma, etc. If we study the novels of Bhabani Bhattacharya, Raja Rao, Mulk Raj Anand, R.K. Narayan and other established novelists writing in English we can easily trace out the use of Indian words in Indian English. These Indian words represent Indian heritage of culture and philosophical life.

(vi) Indian English has specific socio-linguistic rules of address. If we study the Indian English discourses, we can find out the individulistic trends of rules of address. Indian English is a socio-linguistic reality today. Localisation of the global code for satisfying socio-cultural needs is a must.

Social Aspects of Language

EXERCISES

1. Look at the following sentences. Say whether they are acceptable. If a sentence is unacceptable, say why it is so.
   1. I aren't bothered.
      I amn't bothered.
      I ain't bothered.
   2. I'm right, aren't I?
   3. We've got to finish the job by next week or we'll be getting a bad reputation.
   4. He met up with Sourav in Boston.
   5. Let he and I do it—we can manage between us.
   6. I am thinking about it.
   7. I am loving him.
   8. I were going down the lane.
   9. I dislike to read Romantic Literature.
   10. We discussed about our nagging brother.
2. (a) What is discourse analysis? What are the factors that go into discourses?
   (b) What is 'Indian English'? Discuss some of the features of 'Indian English'.

MAIN BRANCHES OF LINGUISTICS

Linguistics has several main branches (as shown in Fig. X) like Stylistics, Socio-linguistics, Applied linguistics, Comparative linguistics, Computational linguistics and Psycho linguistics. The branches have become more numerous over the years.

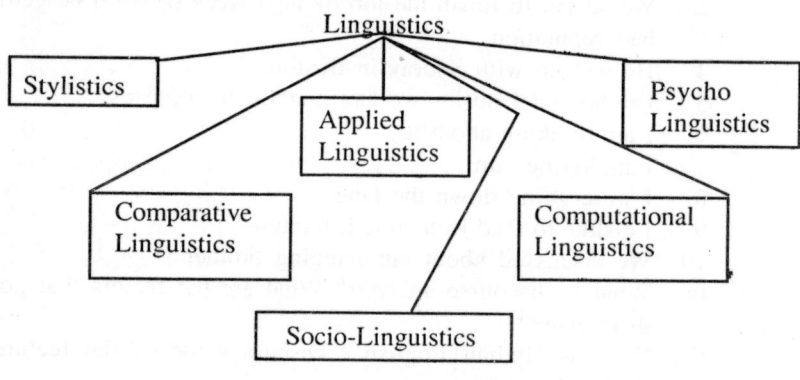

Fig. X

Stylistics—Stylistics tries to make use of the new insights of theories in Linguistics to study the language of literature. Actually, stylistics is the linguistic study of literature. Some rudimentary linguistic concepts are responsible for stylistic analysis. For example—foregrounding, which is a technique often been equated orthographic deviation as in William Blake's *Tyger* (not 'Tiger'), deviation in punctuation, morphological deviation and so on. The deviations are also possible in syntax. W.H. Auden's poem *The Wanderer* exhibits the "subjectless, articleless" (Leech) style suggesting a coordinated view of life. The syntactic deviation may often consist in the inversion of the general word order. For example,

"Him the Almighty power"

[*Paradise Lost*, Book-I, 11 : 44]

Lexical collocation, colligation, repetition, shift of register are some of the styles used in stylistic analysis.

Psycho-Linguistics—"Psycho-linguistics is the study of the mental process underlying the planning, production, perception and comprehension of speech." (Finch). Psycho-Linguistics has close links with the Clinical

Main Branches of Linguistics

Linguistics and Aphasiology. Language is considered as a psycho-linguistic activity (by some linguists). Psycho-Linguistics also has reference to the stages of language acquisition :

Vegetative sounds → Cooing → Vocal play
Two-word-stage ← single words ← Babbling
↓
Telegraphic sentence → Full sentence → bring out
↓
Adult stage

Psycho-linguistics also concerns with human brain and human mind. It is sometimes referred to as the "Psychology if Language".

Socio-linguistics—Socio-linguistics is the study of language in relation to society. It is a blend of Sociology and Linguistics. This branch of Linguistics is often been termed as 'Sociology of Language'. Language is a socio-individual event. Socio-linguistics is a reaction against the Chomskyan School which proposed the so-called 'armchair' methods of Generative Linguistics. Socio-linguists are interested in 'real speech that goes into the process of verbal communication. the social variables influence speech in particular. The language user is himself a member of a society. His personal factors like age, sex. race, nationality, socio-political background, family status etc., play crucial roles in language use. The sociolinguists collect data by random sampling of 'langue' of people. The informants are the members of the society, 'style shifting', 'code switching', 'code mixing', 'sociolet', 'idiolet', 'aborated code', 'restricted code', 'pidgins', 'preoles', 'formal standard', 'informal standard'—all these terms are socio-linguistic terms. 'Register' is also a socio-linguistic term. It refers to a socially contextually, defined style of language.

'Register' is also related to degrees of formality of language use. Therefore, business letters are written in formal register where as when we write to our parents we follow informal register. Words in a language should be used appropriately, keeping in mind the context (in which a particular word is to be selected). For example, "home" :

abode (poetic situation)
doss (slang use)
home (main word)
domicile (official use)
residence (formal use)
dwelling (formal/journalistic use)

Like 'code switching' and 'style shifting' 'register shifting' is also possible. But, this very fact comes under the head—'style shifting'. 'Register-borrowing' is a socio-linguistic reality. Martin Joos (in 1962) describes five basic registers which people use in day to day communication :

(i) *Formal*—informative as well as discursive.
Example—as used in the lecture.

(ii) *Consulative*—conversing with a stranger.
(iii) *Intimate*—used between people who are close to each other for years.
(iv) *Casual*—used in friendly conversations.
(v) *Frozen*—Fixed expressions as used in funeral sevices or scriptures.

Man's use of language varies with the situation—at the College or University classrooms, at home, at office, in the market and so on. Similarly, man's language varies due to geographical reasons. Variability on geographical reasons is called dialectal. When social dimension goes into language variation, it is called sociolectal. These two-dimensional variability can be illustrated in the following way:

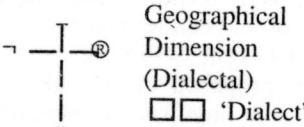

Geographical
Dimension
(Dialectal)
□□ 'Dialect'

Sociolectal ('Sociolect')

When a person talks, he varies his speech (performance) in both sociological and the geographical dimensions in relations with specific social contexts. According to Gumperz (1971), we can map/plot the specific linguistics usage of any individual within a social group.

Idiolect—Idiolect is the speech habits of an individual. Each of us has specific idiolect. The socio-linguists trace out the idiolect with the help of recurring feature that marks his/her sppech.

Isogloss—Isogloss is an imaginary line drawn on a map to mark the boundary of an area where a particular linguistic feature is used. This imaginary boundary line is also known as dialect boundary.

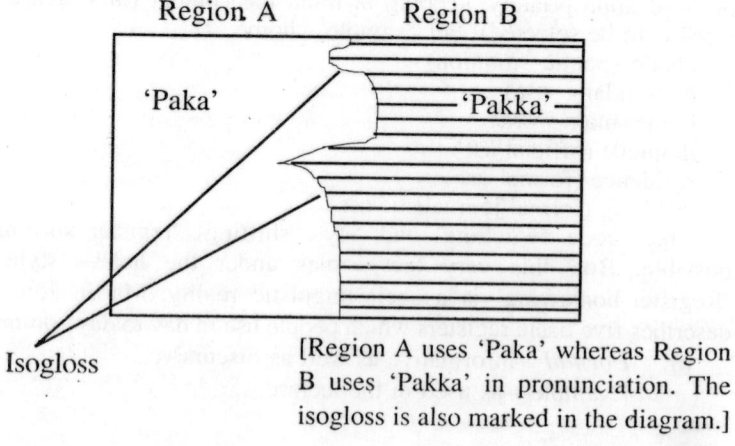

[Region A uses 'Paka' whereas Region B uses 'Pakka' in pronunciation. The isogloss is also marked in the diagram.]

Socio-linguistics merges into the related areas of Stylistics and Discourse Analysis. Ethnomethodology (a study of the conventions of the conversations such as turn-taking, off-topic reference) and Ethonography of communication is connected with style. Socio-linguistic rules of address is also an area where people differ due to different customs and traditions of the countries and nationalities.

Language Registers—Language registers decide the nature of the language one has to use in either an available or given situation and context. Language registers are governed by suitable and proper jargon, terminology or vocabulary. Language Registers belong to various disciplines. For example :

(i) **Legal Register** for using the language of lawer courts, civil, criminal and revenue cases, consumer court case. The human rights and constitutional obligations are the places for Legal Register.

(ii) **Religious Register** for temples, mosques, churches, Gurudwara and such other places of worship and for religious books, problems, events, festivals, occasions, rites and rituals.

(iii) **Medical Register** for using in hospitals talking to doctors and patients, about medicines, treatments, discussions on diseases and investigations, etc.

Applied Linguistics

Jacques Derrida's assertion that reality is a mere linguistic construct has brought a widespread scepticism about the study of literature, as teachers of English understand it. It is argued that the text (literary/verbal) has no existence as an "object exterior to the psyche and history of the man who interprets it." (Barthes 1972 : 72) The reader of the text may be any reader (from any culture / code) from now to the end of an infinite number of meanings. Since "meaning is irrecoverable, the responsibility to be correct does not arise". (Das 2003 : 41)

It is the study of language teaching. Language teaching involves following factors :

(i) The objectives of teaching language differ according to the levels of teaching. Objectives in pedagogy derive out of the needs analysis of the students.
(ii) Teaching methodology is also an important factor. The classroom teacher can opt for Grammar Translation method, Direct method, Communicative method and so on.
(iii) Curricula of the language course plays a crucial role in Language Teaching. The syllabus must be graded. And it must meet the demands of the students.
(iv) Medium of instruction is another pedagogical issue. Sometimes teachers like to translate the Target Language (TL) to make things acceptable for the students.

(v) Teaching materials are essential in teaching language, which is a highly skilled job. The age-old blackboard tradition is still there. Now, a classroom teacher can use Flash cards, Projector, Gramophone, Language Laboratory, Tape Recorder or even a Computer in the classroom. Motion Pictures are used in classroom instruction too. It combines pictures with movement, colour and sound. Radio and Televisions are often used in the classroom. They are powerful aids of teaching. Actually, all depends on the willingness from the part of the teacher. The availability of these aids of teaching in a developing country like India, may be a dream. But, we all need to be 'creative' to meet something 'creative' in the process.

(vi) Evaluation ('summative' or 'formative') is employed to test the exit-behaviour of the learners. And there must be a definite progress of the learner from the initial behaviour to the exit behaviour.

(vii) The classroom teacher is the link between the entire language course and the learners. He is the real performer. He makes use of the available resources.

There are many other issues of language teaching. There are four skills of language learning : Speaking, Writing, Listening and Reading. Teaching language aims at satisfying all these four skills. Language teaching has been changed over the years. Not the focus of Language Teaching has been shifted from 'teaching' to 'learning'.

Quality in Teaching : The term, 'Quality' reminds us arête (Gk.), which means 'Excellence of function'. Quality in teaching involves planning, delivering and evaluating the optimum curriculum for individual pupil in the context of a range of learners. A good teacher must be a reflective practitioner. Since the tasks facing teachers are constantly to be seeking ways to inprove their practice. 'Standard', 'professional', 'competence', 'accountability' and 'appraisal' are part of the rhetoric of quality teaching. A 'quality' teacher must develop the craft skills (pedagogic).

APPLICATION OF LINGUISTICS IN LITERARY DISCOURSE

The Discourse of Resistance: A Study of Arundhati Roy's *The God of Small Things*

The colonial discourse of power envisages the twin processes of subversion of the cultural milieu of the colonised and direct or indirect imposition of the coloniser's language upon the latter. The post-colonial novelists in many diglossic socio-cultural contexts like Africa, Australia and India want to subvert these twin processes. This twin processes pave an open-ended space to determine whether such a 'decolonising' project is 'false' and 'ultimately contradictory':

> It is false because it confuses usage with property in its view of meaning, and it is ultimately contradictory, since, of it is asserted that words do have some essential cultural essence not subject to changing usage, the post-colonial literatures of English, predicted upon this very changing usage, could not have come into being. (Ashcroft *et al* 1989: 53)

> The post colonial cross-cultural texts establish a 'now devised post-colonial variety of English' (Chakraborty 2000: 09):

> The post-colonial texts of the diglossic societies [...] use a language which is different from the language of power and give the writer an amplitude of freedom which conformity to the metropolitan / standard variety so far denied.

'Postcolonialism' becomes a tool of cultural politics and literature in the hands of the authors and politicians who belong to the countries that were previously in the hold of colonisers. However, 'Postcolonialism' is a contested term that is deciphered for further extension in meaning, scope and approach. The given definitions highlight one or the other aspect of 'Postcolonialism'. But all the postcolonial theorists harp on the point that though actual colonialism is over, it has its after effects in Postcolonial countries notwithstanding their vigorous political and administrative sovereignty. In simple term, we can define Post-colonialism as a set of theoretical approaches that focus on the direct effects and aftermaths of colonisation. Postcolonialism as an open space in any literature of subjugation or marginalisation marked by a systematic process of cultural domination through the imposition of imperial structures of power. Postcolonialism is implicit in the discourses of colonialism. Hence, Postcolonialism studies the after effects of response and resistance to the legacy of colonialism in the field of philosophy and literature and presents the identity of the colonised and its culture representing the un-represented and voicing the un-voiced with a set of codes not available in colonial grammar. The Australian mainstream post colonial writers Bill Ashcroft, Gareth Griffiths, and Helen Tiffin argue in 1989 in their seminal book, *The Empire Writes Back* that theory and practice in Post-Colonial Literatures, that the post-colonial era began from the point of colonisation itself. They argue that the writing back has started even before the independence of the colonised countries. Even in the post-colonial society colonialism continues in different forms.

Aijaz Ahamad in his famous article *The Politics of Literary Post-coloniality* shows the differences of opinion regarding the 'language of the Empire' :

> [...] Post colonial writers who write in the language of the Empire are marked off as traitors to the cause of a reconstructive postcolonialism [...] Postcolonial writers compose under the shadow of 'death'.

English virtually the official language of India; 40 percent of all publishing in India is done in English, as more English speakers are said to reside in India today than in Britain. **Indian** (Variety of) **English** is a Sociolinguistic reality and an accepted linguistic code these days. Indian English is different from the standard English since the Indians look at the world in a particular way which is very different from the native speakers of English.

The linguistic creativity and resourcefulness of the post-colonial writers do not create cultural difference or linguistic isolation. The postcolonial writers write for a cultural compromise through the artistic alchemy of so-called standard language of the empire and the indigenous / native / local variety as if the queen wearing *bindi*.

The God of Small things (1997) begins with the brooding month of May in Ayemenem, Kerala and ends with Velutha leaning on the mangosteem tree watching Ammu, a Syrian Christian, walk away with the promise to 'Naaley'. Throughout the three hundred and thirty nine pages of this Booker Award winning book, Kerala remains a vibrant and throbbing presence. Various folk habits, customs and social activities build up the composite background of the Kerala culture. Arundhati Roy creates a world peopled with a variegated assortment of characters. A paedophile, callow adults, de-moralised parents, the half-awake Estha – one of the Siamese twins with a difference, always washing or walking – Baby Kochamma who "had lived her life backwards", the wife – beating Pappachi and his victim Mammachi – each one of these characters is unusual or extraordinary in some way. The novel serves as a "mirror to the cultural milieu of India in the last half-a-century with its uniqueness and variety" (Pinto 2002:149). *The God of Small Things*, a work of highly conscious art, is conscious not least of its linguistic ambivalence. It takes place in India's southern most state of Kerala, where the local language is Malayalam.

Application of Linguistics in Literary Discourse

The God of Small Things has been appreciated for its verbal wizardry and verbal exuberance. Arundhati Roy's *The God of Small Things* constantly foregrounds the conventional and accepted rules of language. She writes in an iconoclastic style truly different from that of other Indo-English novelists. Her style doesn't match with Mulk Raj Anand's works filled with Punjabi expletives and frippery translated into English or Bhabani Bhattacharya's style in transcreation of vernacular discourses into English. Arundhati Roy writes "with a linguistic exuberance which lends a flavour and colour, though artificial of its own to the entire novel" (Nityanandam 1999: 114). Her novel has been scrutinised negatively again and again for her over-writing, of typographical coyness, various types of linguistic deviations (creativity?) and self-indulgence.

Arundhati Roy's *linguistic deviation* includes *syntactical deviation morphological deviation, punctuational deviation,* and *stylistic deviation.* There are plenty of non-sentences in the novel. Non-sentences do not S-V-O pattern:

> Fathers, Mangoes, spit
> All the way to Cochin.(82)
> Collapsed fountains.
> Flattened puffs.(172)
> Sicksweet. Like old roses on a breeze. (06)
> Thirty-one
> Not old.
> Not young.
> But a viable die-able age. (03)

This syntactical deviation is eye-catching. No linguistic rule can explain Arundhati Roy's linguistic experimentations. She doesn't bother for syntactical order of the constituents of a so-called sentence. The novel abounds in single word sentences, and paragraphs, which apparently seem to be un-English:

> Entered.
> Lived. (78)
> Wild. Sick. Sad. (159)
> Gate.
> Road.
> Stones.
> Sky.
> Rain. (285)
> Out.
> In.
> And lifted its leg.
> Up.
> Down. (293)
> Slimy. Warty. Croaking. (187)

According to Indira Nityanandam (1999: 144), Arundhati Roy's linguistic deviation "is overdone even when we accept the writer's right to poetic license." Arundhati Roy uses repetition of words, phrases, and sentences as a device of intensification which are sociolinguistically true to communicative discourse in India. She makes use of *Indian reduplication* to its maximum:

> One beach – coloured.
> One brown.
> One Loved.
> One loved a little less. (186)

He loved them. He loved her (Julie Andrews), she loved him, they loved the children, the children loved them. (105)

The God of Small Things abounds in *morphological deviations*. Telescoping is the process of forming new words by combining two or more terms into one. It is a primitive process of word formation in the English language. The *God of Small Things* abounds in *telescoped* (become compressed forcibly) words:

> 'Thiswayandthat' (107)
> (has become compressed forcibly from "This way and that")
> 'Finethankyou,' (145)
> (has become compressed forcibly from 'Fine thank you')
> 'Ofcourseofcourse' (109)
> (has become compressed forcibly from 'Of course of course')
> 'Bluegreyblue' (238)
> (has become compressed forcibly from 'Blue grey blue')
> 'pleasetomeetyou' (212)
> (has become compressed forcibly from 'please to meet you')

Arundhati Roy uses these *nonce-words* as a part of *neologism. Neologism* (creating new words) is not a violation of the lexical rule. It is a fertile process of word-formation. Geoffrey N. Leech in his famous book. *A linguistic Guide to English Poetry* (1969: 78) defends the poet's right to "ignore the rules and conventions generally observed by the users and conventions generally observed by the users of that language." Arundhati Roy's punctuations in the novel transgress the orthodox boundaries of acceptability. She forcibly breaks the traditional format of punctuations in order to make the crusade against the established practice of the colonizer's code. We can cite a few *punctuational deviations* below:

> *They* were or ever thought *they'd* be.
> Ever.
> Their lives have a size and shape now.
> Estha has his and Rahel hers. (03)

They were opening a bottle.
Or shutting a tap.
Cracking an egg to make an omelette. (308)

One of her passages in the novel displays an architectural design, which is like the prosaic equivalence to 'pattern poetry'(The term was coined in the 1950s, and in 1956 an international exhibition of pattern poetry was shown in São Paulo(Brazil), inspired by the work of Carlos Drummond de Andrade).

Nictiating
ictiating
titating
itating
tating
ating
ting
ing. (189)

Pattern poetry or shape poetry is poetry in which the typographical (visual) arrangement of words is as important in conveying the intended effect as the conventional elements of the poem, such as meaning of words, rhythm, rhyme and so on. It is sometimes referred to as visual poetry, a term that has evolved to have distinct meaning of its own. This particular style of poetry originated in Alexandria during the third century B.C. Poems under this school are designed as shape for religious art-works, including wing—, axe— and altar—shaped poems. It blurs the boundaries between poetry and visual art.
There are many varieties of pattern poetry that exist:

- Haiku
- Tanka
- Diamante
- Cinquain
- Acrostic

Sometimes, children take a word apart just for the sake of fun out of the process of its disintegration. No rule of grammar can define such *stylistic deviation* satisfactorily. This deviationist approach gives Arundhati Roy's novel's "a bold new look" (Chakraborty 2002: 10)

Nativisation of English is one of the seminal issues of *The God of Small Things*. This *nativisation* is achieved by incorporating stylistic resourcefulness, creating a language variance from the so-called standard variety by interweaving indigenous / regional terms with the conventional English, or by using hybridized words and phrases, unglossed expressions, and syntactical variations. Like other authors writing in English about India and Indians, Arundhati Roy has to grapple with the two-fold stylistic problem of :

a) trying to represent, in English, how Indians converse among themselves in languages other then English, and
b) trying to represent how Indians use English.

Arundhati Roy belongs to a school, which try to interpret India to the English-speaking world ; they highlight those aspect of Indian life and culture which may be of special interest to the English-speaking world, and these include the tempo of Indian speech. Postcolonial methodology addresses centers, difference, totalizing, hegemony and margins as determined by Indian social milieu. The morning of Sophie Mol's arrival, the uncle of Estha and Rahel buys two red roses to welcome his ex-wife and child:

Two roses red.
Fatly.
Fondly. (141)

'Fatly' is used because they see their uncle as a fat man. 'Fondly', is used because they also know that he is exceedingly fond of Sophie Mol and Margaret Kochamma. This technique of Arundhati Roy allows language to embody non-verbal experience. The above quoted monologue transgresses rules of traditional English grammar. "Two roses red" reflects logical anomalies in the syntactical order. Interior monologue is the expression of raw thoughts, which lie nearest to the unconscious. Rahel, who comes back to Aymenem, is a young woman who has grown older and wiser. Now, she journeys down the memory lane to catch up her old association with Ammu:

Thirty-one.
Not old.
Not young.
But a viable die-able age. (03)

In relating Ammu's premature death, Arundhati Roy foregoes traditional commentary and presents it through the isolated and disjointed consciousness of Rahel, without the support of a story-narrator. In other occasion, Estha and Rahel seem to be too young to know about the funeral. In their consciousness Sophie Mol's coffin alone stands out vividly:

Sophie Mol had a special child-sized coffin.
Stain-lined.
Brass handle shined. (04)

The above description photographically presents the blazing structure of the coffin. The above sentences do not follow any rule. They are simply non-sentences. These (non-) sentences are written under the direct influence of the tempo of Malayalam speech.

Kamala Das in her poem *An Introduction* says:

> The language I speak
> Becomes mine, its distortions, its queerness
> All mine, mine alone. It is half English, half
> Indian, funny perhaps, but it is honest
> It is as human as I am human ....

The God of Small Things is written in a style of 'half English, half Indian'. It excludes traditional English from any sociable code of communication, excepting the *hybridized* (as well as *vernacularized*) speech acts of the discourse in *Indian English*. Arundhati Roy makes use of Malayalam words and expressions to provide with a *glocal* (global code in local dress) linguistic experience in a multicultural space:

> *Khando* (can you see)(178, 179)
> *Ickilee* (tickle) (178)
> *Modalali* (master) (271)
> *Keto* ('do you hear?')(70)
> *Pada Patti* ('go dog') (90), etc.

Arundhati Roy also uses the unglossed names of the sea-fishes available in Kerala like 'paliathi', 'poral', 'koori' and 'karimeen'. (203) Malayalam words and expressions are used in hybridized form along with English words and expressions:

> '*Aiyyo kastham*', Velutha said. (177)
> ['Aiyyo kastham', a Malayalam phrase, means 'how sad']
> He kept dropping his packages and saying, '*Ende Deivomay!*'
> 'Eee sadhanangal!' (143)
> [The Malayalam phrase means "My god! These things."]

Sometimes, Arundhati Roy provides with the English translation of the Malayalam sentences for the sake of better comprehensibility of her novel:

> *Avaney kadalamma Kandu poyi.* (220)
> (So mother Ocean rose and took him away.)
> *Pandoru mukhwan muthinu poyi,*
> (Once a fisherman went to sea,)
> *Padinjaram kattathu mungipoyi,* (219)
> (The West Wind blew and swallowed his boat,)

At times, Arundhati Roy's English is reduced to a nonsensical entity. Estha and his sister make a mess of clustering of consonants and vowels. They playfully change "barn owl" into tantalizing child language "Bar Nowl" (193). Some of her words are non existent in the parlance of coloniser's language:

> 'Then offity off', Rahel said. (210)

Possibly, 'offity' is her own creation. Even the Indian readers are bound to stumble at this point. Arundhati Roy "re-pidgins" (Indian) English with her mischievous (innovative?) stylistic experimentations.

Interpersonal rhetoric consists of a set of *maxims*. *Principles* and *maxims* play important role in the description of linguistic meaning of literary textual discourses. Characters of *The God of Small Things* sometimes, strictly follow the *conversational maxims* and sometimes flout these *maxims*. Let us cite some examples of adherence of *agreement maxim*:

> 'Then sandpaper', Estha said 'Then Polish'.
> 'Then oars', Rahel said.
> 'The pars', Estha agreed.

Kuttappen assures Rahel and Estha that a vallom leak is not hard enough to mend. Kuttappen suggests his idea to mend the leak. Estha and Rahel mention the further process one by one. They seem to be agreed on future steps about the operation. In another occasion, Estha feels stomach-ailment. He feels 'vomity'. Ammu becomes worried to see him in this condition. Ammu seeks his permission to make him feel better. Estha agrees with Ammu:

> 'Just feeling or d' you want to?' Ammu's voice was worried.
> 'Don't know'.
> 'Shall we go and try? – Ammu said, 'It'll make you feel better'.
> Okay? Okay. (107)'

There is hardly any disagreement among the participants in the above conversation. Ammu comes forward to make Estha feel better. Estha agrees on the subject. In the process, they follow the *maxim of agreement*. There are examples of violation of the *agreement maxim* too. Chacko and Ammu have two different sets of opinion regarding 'going to see *The Sound of Music*'. Chacko thinks it as an 'extended exercise in Anglophilia.' Ammu does not take it seriously. For him, it is a natural thing. Chacko expresses his resentment at Ammu in a loud voice:

> Chacko said that going to see the *Sound of Music* was an extended exercise in Anglophilia. Ammu said, 'Oh come on, the whole world goes to see *The Sound of Music*. It's World Hit.'
> 'Nevertheless. My dear.' Chacko said in his reading aloud voice. 'Never. The. Less.' (55)

The characters in *The God of Small Things* often prove to be more informative than they are required to be. Sometimes the purpose of a person's extra-information is to convince the readers. That is what seemed to be the intention of Rahel in the following conversation:

> Has Chacko Saar's Mol come? Kuttappen asked.

'Must have,' Rahel said laconically.
'Where's she?'
'Who knows? Must be around somewhere. We don't know.'
'Will you bring her here for me to see?'
'Can't,' Rahel said.
'Why not?'
'She has to stay indoors, She's very delicate. If she gets dirty she'll die.'
'I see.'
'We not allowed to bring her here ... and anyway, there's nothing to *see*,' Rahel assured Kuttappen. 'She has hair, legs, teeth – you know – the usual ... only she's a little tall.' (209-210)

In the above conversation, Rahel should have stopped without describing Chacko Saar's Mol's physical appearance in details which is not important in the ongoing discourse. In the process, Rahel violets the *quantity maxim* in the siciolinguistic interpersonal rhetoric.

The God of Small Things explores some of the most discerning critical responses related to postcolonialism, raising some seminal issues as to how races are linked with nations, and how the imprisoned space liberates the postcolonial textual space in the horizontality of events chained in the discourse of resistance :

"The gap which opens between the experience of sociological place and the language available to experience/describe it forms the matrix of postcolonial texts. Language question in postcolonial literature is a cultural action based upon the stimulus response of the individuals to their environment."(Sarangi 2007: vi)

The desire of today's anti-colonial language researcher is to retrieve a history of the regional language in the hybridised linguistic space in a multilingual country where the response and the interaction are dictated on the composition of society's formulation.

NOTE:

The edition of the text I quote is :

Roy, Arundhati. *The God of Small Things*,New Delhi:Indialnk,1997.
Page Numbers within brackets indicate page references of the actual primary text.

WORKS CITED

Ahamad, Aijaz, "The Politics of Literary Post-coloniality". Ed.Mongia P. *Contemporary Postcolonial Theory*, New Delhi: O.U.P.,1983 (rpt.1997). 277.

Ashcroft, B., Griffiths, G. and Tiffin, H. *The Empire Writes Back*, London : Routledge,1989, 53-54.

Chakraborty, S. "Myth and Reality: Arundhati Roy's Use of Language in *The God of Small Things*." The Quest, Vol.16., No.1, Ranchi, June 2002, 9-14.

Das, Kamala. 'An Introduction', *Summer in Calcutta*, Paranjape Makarand (ed.), 1965. 141.

Leech, G.N *A Linguistic Guide to English Poetry*, Harlow: Longman, 1969, 78.

Nityanandam,Indira , *"The God of Small Things"* : A Linguistic Experiment.

Roy," *Explorations: Arundhati Roy's The God of Small Things*, New, Delhi: Indialnk, 1997

Pinto, R., "The God of Small Things: The Cultural Milieu" *Indian Writing in English.*

(Ed.) Prasad, A.N., New Delhi: Sarup and Sons, 2002, 149.

Sarangi, Jaydeep, *Presentations of Postcolonialism : New Orientations*, New Delhi: Authorspress, 2007, "Preface"(vi).

LANGUAGE IN EDUCATION POLICY SINCE INDEPENDENCE

India's independence from British rule in 1947 brought about a number of fundamental changes in language policy. While the language policies during the colonial period dealt essentially with the role of English vis-a-vis the "vernacular" languages, the mandated use of Hindi as the official language brought a new participant into the picture: the constitutional safeguards given to linguistic minorities (though they were only recommendatory and not directive) added yet another element to be reckoned with in formulating a language-in-education policy.

Complicating this task was the federal structure of government adopted in the Constitution, which designed education as "State" (not federal) subject. The Central Government appointed a series expert committees and commissions whose recommendations were debated, passionately and often violently, in the public forums. The most important of these commissions and their major recommendations are summarised below (India 1953, 1959, Kothari 1970) :

(1) The Conferences of the Vice Chancellors of Universities (1948), recommended the replacement of English by Indian languages (primarily the major regional languages) as the medium of instruction at the university level within (the unrealistically short period of) five years. (It is interesting to note that the goal has not been achieved even 40 years after the recommendation was made—so much for the effectiveness of committees.)

(2) The Conference of the Education Ministers of the States (1948), recommended the adoption of the mother tongue as the medium of instruction at the primary and secondary school levels, with the state language when it differed from the mother tongue to be studied as a compulsory subject.

(3) The University Education Commission (1949) recommended that students at the secondary and university levels should know three languages, namely the regional language, the link language—Hindi and English.

(4) The Secondary Education Commission (known as the Mudaliar Commission, after its Chairman) (1952), endorsed the recommendation of the education ministers' conference and additionally, it recommended the study at least two other languages, e.g., Hindi and English, at the higher primary level (grades through 8).

(5) The English Review Committees (known after its chairman as the Kunzru Committee, appointed by the Univeristy Grants Commission in 1955) emphasized the need to "go slow" on the switch over to regional language as media of instruction at the university level,

and urged the need for the continued study of English by all university students even after the switch in the media.
(6) The Central Advisory Board of Education (1957), suggested what has come to be known as the Three Language Formula which was adopted by the Conference of State Chief Ministers in 1961. This policy recommended the study of (i) the regional language, (ii) Hindi in non-Hindi areas and any other Indian language in the Hindi area, and (iii) English or any other modern European language.
(7) The Education Commission (also known as the Kothari Commission, after its Chairman) (1964-66), looked into the problems faced by the states in implementing the Three Language Formula, and recommended a 'modified, graduaisted" Three Language Formula, which won general (though by no means unanimous, see below) acceptance. This is the language policy currently in force in most of India. (For a more detailed discussion, see K. Sridhar 1989).

Aims and Objectives of Teaching of English in Colleges

The aims and objectives have to be formulated in the light of what we perceive our needs for English to be, at both the national and the indiviudal levels.

At the national level, English must serve as our 'window on the world'—as the language in which nearly contemporary knowledge is accessible. As the language of science and technology, English will be important for industrial and economic development. It will function as the 'language of development', our scientists, technologists, engineers, doctors, etc. must be able not only to have access to professional literature in English but also to contribute to it, and to communicate with their counterparts in other parts. The continuation of English seems important if our science and technology are to be truly international.

As the associate official language, the de facto 'link language' the language favoured by the UPSC, the legal and the banking systems, trade and commerce and defence, English will have important functions to serve internally—in addition to its role as our 'window on the world'.

English may continue to be the medium of instruction in several faculties at the college level.

Where the medium of instruction is to be some language other than English, the 'library language' function of English will have to be stressed.

At the individual level, English will still serve as 'the language of opportunity' ; any individual seeking socio-economic advancement will find ability in English as the asset.

It is clear, therefore, that English will have important functions in communications of diverse types. The skills of communication, oral as well as written, both expressive and receptive, will continue to be at a premium, and teaching will have to try to impart a certain minimal competence in these skills.

It is important, however, that we should be able to identify the English requirements of various groups of students precisely, and try to provide for each such group the pattern of instruction which will be relevant to its needs.

SOME KEY TERMS

Second Language (SL, TL, L2, L3)

'Second' language normally stands as a cover term for any language other than the first language learned by a given learner or group of learners ca) irrespective of the type of learning enviornment and cb) irrespective of the number of other non-native languages possessed by the learner. This includes both 'foreign' languages (for example, French as a foreign language for Austrians) and languages which are not one's mother tongue but are nevertheless spoken regularly in one's own community (for example, French for English-speaking Canadians). 'Second' seems better than definitions such as 'secondary' or non-native' which imply lower status, 'Second language' is often abbreviated to 'L2' (as opposed to 'L1'—the mother tongue). An L2, then, means, unless otherwise specified, a particular 'non-native language under discussion', that is, the so-called 'target' language (TL). In certain circumstances, the more literal terms L3, L4, etc., may be also used as in 'the influence of a learner's L2 German upon her L3 Dutch'. Second language research is to be interpreted as covering a large area, including psychological, neurological, pragmatic and sociological aspects of L2 development and L2 use.

Interlanguage (IL)

IL most generally refers to the systematic linguistic behaviour of learners of a second or other language; in other words, learners of non-native languages. It calls our attention to the possibility of viewing learner language such as 'the Finnish of English learners of Finnish', for example, as possessing systematic features which can be studied in their own right. The idea is that they are not merely imperfect reflections of some norm in this particular case that norm would be 'educated native speaker Finnish'.

The 'language' part of the term 'interlanguage' suggests this idea of an autonomous linguistic system while the 'inter' of 'interlanguage' reminds us that this version of Finnish is supposed to be a half-way house, an intermediate stage in the user's linguistic development. In using the term 'interlanguage' as linguistic development. In using the term 'interlanguage' as a noun, it is best to keep to the behavioral definition. Essentially this means the language events that you can actually observe and record.

It is not the invisible language system: This must exist somewhere in the mind of the user but we cannot perceive it directed. Interlanguage is, as it were, the bees and beehives we can see, touch, hear and smell and not the principles that dictate their shape and determine all the fascinating activities that we can observe. In this way we can talk about given samples of 'interlanguage' and speculate about the 'interlanguage system' that underlies it.

The terms 'interlanguage' and 'learner language' will be used interchangeably, without denying their sociological value, it can be said tha interlanguage studies typically focus on the linguistic and psychological aspects of second language research. For the linguistic and mental systems underlying interlanguage terms such as 'interlanguage system' or 'interlanguage grammar' or 'interlanguage lexicon' will be employed.

Strategy

'Strategy' is a word which invokes the idea of general on business executives planning their next move. The term is used in a variety of ways and its precise meanings are sometimes difficult to ascertain. Learners are often said to adopt strategies to cope with the business of handling non-native languages, for examples 'learning strategies' or 'communicative strategies'. Strategies have to do with 'how to learn X' or 'how to communicate X' and the term 'strategy' as used in the literature, should be understood as a systematic approach to a task :

(a) Whether or not the language user is actually consciously aware of applying the strategy in a given context ;

(b) Whether that strategy is part of a stable repertoire of problem solving techniques or whether it is a sudden adhoc invention which the learner, pressed for time, say, devises on the spur of the moment ;

(c) Whether the idea behind the strategy is to facilitate acquistion, i.e., further the development of the learner's knowledge and proficiency in L2, or whether it is purely and simply designed to facilitate communication at a given moment in time.

To take a couple of examples, a subconscious learning strategy would be when the learner, without thinking, uses mother tongue knowledge to create forms in another language (for example, automatically adopting mother tongue word order in L2 questions). A conscious communicative strategy would be when a learner resorts to a gesture or invents a word on the spot which he or she knows to be incorrect but which serves to convey the intended meaning.

METHODS OF TEACHING ENGLISH

GRAMMAR AND TRANSLATION METHOD

The main principles of this method are
(i) Rules of Grammar are given priority over the actual use of the language.
(ii) Words, phrases, sentences and sequences are interpreted and translated by using suitable equivalents and correct grammar.
(iii) The learner learns the target language(TL) through the mother tongue.
(iv) It is based on Grammatical rules and learners have to operate then for correct translation.

Merits
(i) It is convenient for teachers.
(ii) Learning material is easy to prepare.
(iii) Mother tongue is available for assistance.
(iv) Translation and interpretation skills are developed.

Demerits
(i) Speech efficiency is neglected.
(ii) Language learning process is slow.
(iii) Students always have to think first in the mother tongue.
(iv) It tells upon the memory of the learner to remember rules and use them correctly.
(v) Students form the habit of translating literally.

The Bilingual Method
Professor C.J. Dodson of Wales (U.K.) devised this method to facilitate learners of English by assisting them with the judicious use of their mother tongue.

The main principles of this method are:
(i) Mother tongue is used judiciously.
(ii) Literary translations are not allowed in this method.
(iii) In this method complete sentences, sequences and paragraphs are used rather than isolated words and half or broken sentences.

Merits
(i) The learner gets frequent opportunities for practice in English.
(ii) Two languages together are used, therefore there is no less of communication.
(iii) Difficult words, sentences, utterance etc., are made easy with the assistance of the mother tongue.

Demerits
(i) Grammatical concepts are not formed.
(ii) Free interations are not encouraged.
(iii) Learner always tries to depend on the mother tongue's help.
(iv) Teachers activity dominates and students are involved when the teacher wants to do so.

The Direct Method

The Direct Method is also called the 'Natural Method'.

The main principles of this methods are:
(i) It exposes the students directly to the spoken English./ It encourages students to develop good speech habit right from the beginning.
(ii) Oral-drills and talk situations are created.
(iii) Translation is totally banned.
(iv) Formal grammar is not taught. The learners learn grammar through inductive approach.

Merits
(i) The child learns English like his / her mother tongue.
(ii) The child develops natural fluency in English through direct interaction.
(iii) Quick learning is possible.
(iv) The child learns English in a natural and familiar setting.

Demerits
(i) It requires very efficient teachers with good command on English.
(ii) Teachers must know the sound, strees and intonation system of English in order to speak English with correct and acceptable pronunciation and rhythm.
(iii) It is very expensive as it requires a lot of objects and audio-visual or other teacher-learning aids.
(iv) As the medium of instruction in other subjects is not English, the learner gets limited time for speaking in English.

Principles of Communicative Methodology

The focus of English language teaching has shifted from *'teaching'* to *'learning'*. The recent interest is more on 'what should be taught' than 'how things should be presented in the 'classroom situation' (in broader sense). The majority of researchers and course writers pay more to the content of the language programme rather than the ways in which this content should be taught.

Communicative methodology is still unknown to a large 'mass'. But this is being debated. Nowadays teacher or learners often use 'Role Play'. What is it if not communicative? It's an isolated teachnique. In a consistent methodology there should be objective-specific procedures and activities, related to techniques. In this context some terms demand explanations. By *'method'* we mean overall means of achieving the general objectives of a course, carried out with a set of techniques. By 'procedure' we mean some techniques to ensure the learners to lead them to *'success'*.

Before going deep into communicative method let us distinguish *National Syllabus* and *Communicative Methodology*. National syllabus aims at language forms—just as a grammatically based course is. It does not lead to communicative situation. It does not guarantee doing so. But communication is more than simple structures of language. It involves a lot of activities rather than only knowing the formal aspects of language. The functional textbooks highlight the formal aspect, not the communicative aspect. Students learn language to make communication possible. Therefore, they need a guarantee. Now, let us discuss what a communicative method may be:

Principle One: Making sure what we are doing
From teachers point of view, one has to be sure of what he is doing. And from the learners point of view, they should ask, "Why am I learning this?" "What am I learning to do?" Every lesson should start with some kind of activities such as a listening lesson may begin with a weather forecast on the radio; in speaking it may be asking for directions in a strange city. While doing so, the instructions should be clear. And every lesson should end with the learner being able to judge himself and re-can make a point that 'he can do something' which 'he could not at the beginning of the lesson.' This has to be communicatively useful (for a learner).

Actually, activities should be related to the performance of some real and specific task in the foreign language. It may be pattern drilling or role play but the tasks and activities should lead to 'communication possible'.

Principle Two: The whole is more than the sum of the parts
Communication is a dynamic and ever-growing phenomenon. It needs the understanding of the whole thing. In a discourse, where two interlocutors are talking, one has to remain silent while the other person talking. The 'silent' interlocutor reacts only when the other man stops. So that he can grab the whole rather than the part of the discourse.

Principle three: The processes are as important as the forms
Methods aiming at developing the ability of students to communicate in a foreign language reflect the processes of communication, so that practice of the forms of the target language can take place within communicative framework. The processes are :

Information gap—Where there are two persons in a communicative situation, reach each other supplying information. Information gap is possible among social relationships.

It is distinct in the classroom situation where students express their views what the other students do not know. It is regarded as the fundamental to communicative teaching.

Choice—'Choice of what they will say' and 'how they will say' is another crucial factor of communication. For this, the speaker must choose what ideas he wants to express at a given situation, also what linguistic forms are apt to express those ideas in concrete terms. If the choice is open, the speaker may choose any form or any ideas, which may break 'communication' with the other person.

Feedback—When two speakers take part in an interaction, there is normally an aim of some kind in their minds. This is mostly traceable in the classroom situation where learners bring their own ideas with them. While on conversation the interlocutors have expectation that there will be feedback or reaction (verbal) from the listeners. What a person says gets revalued by the other person and spurred to react verbally.

Principle Four: To learn it, to do it
Education ultimately counts learning not teaching. The consequence of the classroom interaction should bad to the effect of learning (for the case of learners). It becomes a learner's responsibility. The teacher only creates the environment for learning. Only the learners are to learn. For this the learners need an environment to do things possible. If the classroom situation is only a monologue situation, Communication fails. For this, the learners are to respond to the given task. Learning should be a two-way process. The system should be as follows :

What   is presented → practised → produced.

And, there should be a gradual development from 'what is presented' and what is 'produced'. In a communication material, there should be effective use of the three things : 'what is presented', 'what is practised' and 'what is produced.'

Principle Five: Mistakes are Not Mistakes
Mistakes *can arise out of two things first the grammatical mistakes, which can arrive at any level and the second is that the student may be forced into activities for which he has not been prepared.* Grammatical mistakes including pronunciation sometimes play crucial in a communication setting. One may think : "What's use of grammar in the process of message coding and decoding?" Sometimes these things carry meaning.

'Mistakes' indicate the process of learning. Communication involves using appropriate forms in appropriate ways. A communicative approach centainly does not provide an easy solution to the problems of mistakes.

Actually, in a communicative approach message is important. *Message related forms should be perfect otherwise, the message may get lost.* The idea should be that there should be flexibility to treat different things as 'mistakes' at different stages in the learning process.

To make things simpler, the language teaching should be divided into two phases—learning the forms and then learning to use them or the application of forms. Actually, there is no room to separate these two compartments which lead to another. They are mutually inclusive.

The classroom teacher is one who should choose the right path, because he is the real man in the teaching-learning situation. He must judge the circumstance and act accordingly. The teacher should take his own priorities in the given situation. And it is a challenge to us to what degree we may reconcile these two aspects of language in the classroom presentation.

I hope it sounds ambiguous because a lot depends upon the 'learners', their background knowledge, their competence as well as the competence of the teacher. All these things are abstract. Nothing sacrosanct there. In a blending, what percent of 'forms' should be blended with what perfect of communicative aspect is an open question to a classroom teacher.

Distance Education

Distance education was born out of pressing social compulsions, dynamics of change, new cultures and new objective-oriented people. It reflects a healthy evolution in the field of education, though in certain ways it may be considered a revolutionary development because it marks a significant break from the centuries old formal or face-to-face teaching / learning system leading to the development of an innovative multi-media teaching / learning system.

Otto Peters is the principal proponent of the idea of distance education as a highly industrialised form of education. Otto Peters, the founding president of the Fernuni versitat, the West Germany Open University, is one of the major theorists of distance education. He laid down four basic propositions :

(i) That this relationship is controlled by the rules to technology as opposed to those of the social order which regulates face-to-face teaching.

(ii) That it is carried on through using language devoid of emotion, as opposed to the interactional speech of classroom instruction.

(iii) That instruction is based on a very limited possibility of analysing students, needs, not, that is, on any expectations arising from personal contact.

(iv) That instructional objectives must, therefore, be achieved by efficiency methods rather than through personal interaction.

Distance education is a form of education in which there is a normal and usually unavoidable physical separation of the teacher and the learner. It is known as 'guided didactic conversation' (coined by Borje Holmberg).
There are some marked features in distance education :
(i) It is self-paced.
(ii) Learners are autonomous.
(iii) Separation of teacher and student.
(iv) It is carried out according to self-selected goals and methods of achieving them.
(v) Teachers are to modify traditional teaching to deal with learner autonomy and distance.

Modern correspondence instruction began in 1840 with Issac Pitaman's Short Hand course for distance students through Penny Post. In USA, the first efforts to organise correspondence instruction were made in 1873. 'Home study', 'Postal tuition', 'Independent Study', 'Correspondence Course' were the early names given to the distance education. Even now terms like campus studies, external studies, non-formal education etc., continue to be in use.

In India, distance education is becoming the order of the day. Due to the financial constrains, students are unable to join face-to-face courses in the Colleges, Institutes or Universities apart from financial constrains, the seats of 'regular courses' are not adequate in numbers so that all who are interested can get in. People who are in different jobs can avail correspondence courses easily whereas in regular mode they cannot. Therefore, the correspondence courses provided by the Institutes like Indira Gandhi National University, Vidyasagar University, Madurai Kamraj University, Burdwan University, Central Institute of English and Foreign Languages (Hyderabad), etc. are of great demand. So, the thought is 'time is precious'. Don't sit idle. Register your name in the course you want. Do the course with fair degree of seriousness. Make yourself ready for the changing demands of the time. The motto is : "Make others job difficult to defeat you. Reach your set goal. Get away with the course. And enjoy lifelong benefits of the course."

SYLLABUS

At its simplest level a syllabus can be described as a statement: what is to be learnt. It reflects of language and linguistic performance Yalden (1987:87) considers it to be "a summary of the contents to which learners will be exposed. It is an approximation of what will be taught and that it cannot accurately predict what will be learnt." After going through various language theories that have shaped syllabus designs, we realise that a good and complete syllabus should include structure, function, situation, topic and skills. There should be ample scope for feedback and flexibility. The teacher must shift his attention from *form to interaction*.

Syllabus Types

Syllabus is the blueprint of the course. It determines "what should be taught" and "what should not be taught". Teachers deliver lectures on contents of syllabus. Learners find their guidelines in their prescribed syllabus. Syllabus, therefore, is a key term in teaching-learning scenario.

Types of syllabuses

(i) **Grammatical:** A list of grammatical structures, such as the present tense, comparison of adjectives, relative clauses, usually into sections graded according to difficulty and/or/ importance. It is a 'graded' syllabus.

(ii) **Lexical:** A list of lexical items (*Pen, Cat, Come in...*) with associated collocations and idioms, usually divided into graded sections. One such syllabus, based on a corpus (a computerized collection of samples of authentic language) is described in Willis, 1990.

(iii) **Grammatical-lexical:** A very common kind of syllabus: both structures and lexis are specified: either together, in sections that correspond to the units of a course, or in two separate lists.

(iv) **Situational:** These syllabuses take the real-life contexts of language as their basis : Sections would be headed by names of situations or locations such as 'Eating a meal' or 'In the street'.

(v) **Topic-based:** This is rather like the situational syllabus, except that the headings are broadly topic-based, including things like 'Food' or 'The family' ; these usually indicate a fairly clear ser of vocabulary items, which may be specified.

(vi) **Notional:** 'Notions' are concept that language can express. General notions may include 'number', for example, or 'time', 'place', 'colour' ; specific notions look more like vocabulary items : 'man', 'woman', 'afternoon'. For an introduction to the topic of notional syllabuses see Wilkins, 1976.

(vii) **Functional-notional:** Functions are things you can do with language, as distinct from notions you can express : examples are 'identifying', 'denying', 'promising'. Purely functional syllabuses are rare : usually both functions and notions are combined, as for example in Van Ek, 1990.

(viii) **Mixed or 'multi-strand':** Increasingly, modern syllabuses are combining different aspects in order to be maximally comprehensive and helpful to teachers and learners ; in these you may find specification of topics, tasks, functions and notions, as well as grammar and vocabulary.

(ix) **Procedural / Task-based:** These syllabuses specify the learning tasks to be done rather than the language itself or even its meanings. Examples of tasks might be : map reading, doing.

(x) **Process :** It is free from pre-set. Teachers try to negotiate with the contents of process syllabus.

SOME LANGUAGE TEACHING APPROACHES

The Structural Approach:

The structural approach came as a replacement of the Direct Method. It also replaced the New Method or Dr. Michael West's New Method in which there was a great emphasis on reading.

Basic Features of the Structural Approach

(i) The structures are selected and graded.
(ii) It gives importance on oral practice.
(iii) Grammar is derived from the structures.
(iv) Oral drills, vocabulary expansion, presentation of sentences and structures in a given situation are encouraged along with practice in pronunciation.

Objects of the Structural Approach

(i) To enable the students to learn basic structures of English.
(ii) To enrich the vocabulary of the students.
(iii) To improve speech habits of the students with correct pronunciation.
(iv) To enable the students to achieve Mastery level of learning in English through structure.

Advantages

(i) It is a very useful way of teaching as it completely eliminates the use of mother tongue.
(ii) It is useful for a second language learners.
(iii) All the four skills are emphasised.
(iv) Oral drills and pattern practice lead to make learning permanent.

Disadvantages

(i) This approach is not applicable for higher classes and study of literature.
(ii) It is not useful for large classes.
(iii) The ability of creative writing is not adequately developed.
(iv) Selection and gradation is only possible for lower classes.

The Notion of Communication

Communication is a part of the instinct for survival and is achieved through a variety of means. According to Noam Chomsky, when we study human language, we are approaching what some might call the "human essence," the distinctive qualities of mind that are, so far as we know, unique to man. Communication is basically a set of signals. Man uses the most sophisticated system of communication. There is hardly a moment of our waking lives when we don't use words. The possession of language, more than any other attribute, distinguishes humans from other animals. Knowing a language means knowing what sounds are in that language and what sounds are not knowing the sound system of a language includes more than knowing the inventory of sounds: it includes knowing which sounds may start a word, end a word and follow each other. Knowing the sounds and sound patterns in our language constitutes only one part of our linguistic knowledge. In addition, knowing a language is knowing that certain sound sequences signify certain concepts or meaning. Speakers of English know what "bat" means and that it means something different from 'ball' or 'wicket'. Therefore, knowing a language means knowing how to relate sounds and meaning. Knowing a language means being able to produce new sentences never spoken before and to understand sentences never heard before. The linguist Noam Chomsky refers to this ability as part of the "creative aspect" of language use. Not every speaker of a language can create great literature. This creativity shows that language use is not limited to stimulus-response behaviour.

Animals make noises to communicate with the other members of their group. Human beings also makes noises (and / or visual makers) to communicate with other human beings. Animal communication consists of meaningful cries which cannot be analysed into words. Animal communication is closed and context-bound. On the contrary, human communication is open-ended and context-free. Human language is culture-preserving and culture-transmitting. Language is one of the means of contact. Therefore, Descartes said, "Thanks to language, Man becomes Man."

Creativity and resourcefulness are the two most significant aspects of human language. For man, language is indeed a set of signals but certainly not a fixed one. Man makes use of para-languages, body languages, facial expressions and a range of gestures, which form the uniqueness of human language.

How Communication takes place

Communication is the transmission of some information between an addresser and an addressee, based on a system of signals. The addresser encodes some information and produces them in the form of signals (codes). These signals get transmitted through the air particles and it reaches the addressee. The addressee decodes those signals into meaningful information. The human brain (which forms an important part in communication) has an innate capacity for learning and producing language creatively. Language is not a monolithic object. It is a human phenomenon, which is as complex as human relationships in society. Human communication should be studied in relation with human society.

Human communication has three principal modes: tactile, visual and aural. Aural mode relates to speech. In tactile communication an addresser conveys a message to the addressee through touch (by shaking hands by patting on the back). Visual mode involves facial expressions, body language, etc. The study of tactile mode of communication is known as *proxemies* while that of the visual mode is called *kinesics*.

The Communicative Approach

Language is a dynamic (as well as creative) resource for the creation of meaning in all those behaviours which we witness in life. Language is operated through a system of rules. In language, we express, we behave, we act and react and we communicate our thoughts, feelings, emotions and messages. According to David Numan, communicative approach is basically a communicative language teaching approach and it is not a system of rules but it is a system of human interaction through various expressions both in speech and writing.

Basic Features of the Communicative Approach

(i) It is an integration of various approaches.
(ii) It leads to a very high degree of competence in the language as it emphasises all the four skills of the language learning.
(iii) Meaningful and effective communication is always emphasised.
(iv) The learners get enough opportunities to interact and know the social meaning of the language.
(v) The learners develop competence of using language in all circumstances and situations.

Communication is a two-way process. The major hurdles in communication are :
(i) Incorrect pronunciation, stress and intonation in English.
(ii) Ungrammatical use of English.
(iii) Use of broken and incomplete sentences.
(iv) Use of language without relevant contexts.

Communicative Approach, in fact, emphasises on how to overcome these hurdles and how to use the language in appropriate contexts.

Communicative Skills

Communicative skills are basically the skills of the language use. Language use leads to acquire those skills which facilitate the communication.

The four basic language skills contribute to make communication possible. The four basic skills are :

(i) Reading
(ii) Listening
(iii) Speaking, and
(iv) Writing

The communication skills are mainly those skills, which help to communicate through the language successfully with a hundred per cent understanding. These skills can be developed in classrooms by providing maximum practice to learners through a number of already available or created situations and contexts. The communicative skills depend on the following purposes :
- (i) Directions
- (ii) Information
- (iii) Expression with communication
- (iv) Phatic

Phatic function of language is the most used function in day to day life. Phatic expressions do not contain significant information. These are routine, stereotyped expressions. These expressions are face-saving by nature. The phatic expressions are :
- (a) Paying respect saying 'good morning', 'good afternoon', 'good-day', etc.
- (b) Saying 'thank you', 'excuse me', etc.
- (c) Expressions of joy like 'hi', 'hurrah', 'congratulations', etc.
- (d) Maintaining greetings like 'namaskar', 'vanakkam', 'good-morning', etc.

Objectives of Developing Communicative Skills

Communicative skills in English are meant to develop the ability of conversation and communication in all those human situations. The main objectives of the communicative skills are :
- (i) To develop the ability of using English effectively in all real life situations.
- (ii) To develop the ability of selecting right vocabulary for right contexts.
- (iii) To enable the learners to comprehend English effectively.
- (iv) To develop the ability of analysis, discussion, debates, logical arguments, etc.

Reading Skill

Reading is a basic skill for language learning. It is essential in academic and social spheres. Our professional competence rests on our ability to read productively. Reading along with listening is a receptive skill. All reading is not alike. What we mean is that the way we read changes according to individual styles, purposes and the kind of text. The text of reading is any kind of written or printed material. The way we read different texts (written or printed) is always different. It depends on the theme of the text too. The

way we read a newspaper is different from reading a farewell notice in the classroom. Reading is decoding usual symbols, written or printed.
There are four basic techniques of reading :
(i) Extensive Reading.
(ii) Intensive Reading.
(iii) Skimming.
(iv) Scanning.

Extensive Reading : This technique is used to read comparatively longer texts for non-academic purposes. This type of reading is not reading in details. The objective behind this technique is to get a general overview of the text.

Intensive Reading : It is reading in details. Here the stress is on analysis and deeper understanding.

Skimming : It is aimed at getting the basic idea of the text by running our eyes over the text. In this process, we stop when we see something important in the text. Skimming helps us to understand the writers' intension. Skimming is more through activity than scanning.

Scanning : Scanning means search of the text for a particular bit of information. It is actually the retrieval of specific information we want.

Guidelines for developing Reading Skill

(i) Be familiar with the script.
(ii) Deduct the meaning.
(iii) Recognise the unfamiliar words and expressions and deduct the meaning in contexts.
(iv) Understand information which is not explicitly stated.
(v) Follow the linguistic devices and form a general overview of the text.

Listening Skill

Listening is an important language skill and yet the most neglected skill in our classroom. It is neglected because we take it for granted that learners automatically acquire this skill without any special training. Listening is an active process. It can be depicted as follows :

$$\text{Input} \longrightarrow \text{Processing} \longrightarrow \text{Output}$$

By input, we mean the words spoken by the speaker and by output the listener's response, the listener processes the input material before coming out with his output. The input can be processed in two ways :
(i) Bottom-up processing
(ii) Top-down processing

In bottom-up processing, the listener depends only on the incoming input for the meaning of the message. In top-down processing the listener depends on his/her background knowledge for understanding the message.

Types of Listening

According to Adrian Doft, there are two types of listening: *casual listening* and *focussed listening*. In casual listening people tend to listen to something without any particular purpose. On the contrary, in focussed listening the listener is attentive. He concentrates on what the speaker is saying. This kind of listening is also known as "intensive listening".

Guidelines for Developing Listening Skill

(i) Identifying and understanding the intonation pattern and grammar use.
(ii) Reading, summarising and responding properly.
(iii) Recognising the words / phrases and sounds of a language.
(iv) Giving continuous feedback to the speaker.

Writing Skill

Good writing can be identified with the following characteristics:
(i) Good organisation
(ii) Well-knit, logical and systematic presentation
(iii) Lucid and simple style
(iv) Accurate information
(v) Choosing relevant and necessary details
(vi) Avoiding ambiguities in style and presentation

Writings should have definite purpose. It is quite simply the end we are aiming at. It underlines all writing activities. When we write we have to know how it would sound or how others would read it. Choosing the aspect of our topic of writing, we must know how to plan, choice of language, size, etc. The stages of writing involves:

$$\text{Planning} \longrightarrow \text{Writing} \longrightarrow \text{Revising.}$$

Some Model Writing Exercises

Set 1 : Study the following score card and write a newspaper report on it :

Scoreboard

Australia

A Gilchrist c G Jones b Harmison	42
M Hayden c Pietersen b Flintoff	17
R Ponting c Pietersen b Collingwood	14
D Martyn c G Jones b Collingwood	43
A Symonds c Trescothick b Collingwood	6
M Clarke b Collingwood	2
M Hussey not out	46

S Walson c Streuss b Harmison 3
B Lee not out 15
Extras (b2, lb12,w15,nb2) 31
Total (7 wkts, 50 overs)
Fall of wkts : 1/62, 2/68, 3/107, 4/116, 5/120, 6/159, 7/168
Bowling : Gough : 10-1-50-0; Jones : 10-1-28-0; Harmison : 10-0-39-2; Flintoff : 10-0-54-1; Collingwood 10-0-34-4.
Sub : Vikram Solanki replaced Simon Jones after 31 overs.

Set-2 : Study the following newspaper report and prepare an anti-drug slogan.

Drug Lord Held in Delhi

NEW DELHI, July 7 (PTI) : In a major catch, Delhi Police today arrested Sharaft Sheikh, one of the city's most wanted drug lords who allegedly supplied narcotics to Bollywood film stars.

Sheikh (35), who had made crores of rupees from smuggling of drugs, is believed to have sold an imported vehicle to actor Salman Khan.

Owner of a number of property in Delhi and a fleet of eight cars, Sheikh was arrested in Nizamuddin area of South Delhi this morning.

Speaking Skill

Speech comes first in the history of any language community. Speech comes first in the history of any individual. Speech, as the medium of communication is used much more than the medium of writing. But sorry indeed, if we look into our educational system there is hardly any room for the spoken skill. We all talk about four language skills : Spoken, Writing, Listening and Reading but we pay our attention mainly to writing only. We all speak about 'communicative methodology' but we never look into it in the real sense of the phrase. In our Madhyamik (X-level) and H.S. (+ 2) the students are only required to sit for written tests. The same trend continues in our Hons. and M.A. level. Some Universities have included Phonetics for the betterment of the situation. We know students who can write acceptable English but afraid of speaking English. They are not trained anywhere anytime in their life. Whenever these students go outside their respective states, they find life terrible to live in. We cannot get through interviews and GDs without our proficiency in the spoken skill. Students, passing their H.S. (+ 2) take different career options where they badly need the spoken aspect of the language concerned. But do they have any basic knowledge of spoken English? How many of them can differentiate / sit / from / seat / or / sin / from / seen /

in their pronunciation? We are afraid, there may be only a handful of students who can use English in their daily communication. We should not forget that English is the language of trade, commerce and industry. It is the language of translation, interpretation and broadcasting. In every field of life the spoken aspect is a must.

Guidelines for developing the speaking skill

(i) Clarity in pronunciation.
(ii) Correct use of speech sounds, accent and stress.
(iii) Using intonation according to the context.
(iv) Using appropriate style.
(v) Using appropriate sociolinguistic conventions in speech output.
(vi) Developing knowledge of phonetics to produce the right suprasegmental qualities of speech.

Teaching of Literature Through Language

Without language no literature is possible. Literature and language cannot be separated from each other. Michael N. Long in his famous essay on 'A Feeling for Language' says, "Both literature and language teaching involve the development of a feeling for language, of responses to texts in the broadest sense of the word in both written and spoken discourses." Apart from the basic similarities, there are differences between language and literature. Language provides grammatical understanding for use and communication. On the cantrary, literature provides communicative situations through texts. Language is concrete, but literature is abstract. Language belongs to formality and formal mode of speech. Literature belongs to deviations, e.g., slang, dialects, contracts, fields of experience.

Literature is derived from the Latin word *littera* which means letters of the alphabet. Literature is referred to as the matter of imaginative or artistic output. It is a transcript not of means of fact but of fact in its infinitely varied forms. If language is concerned with communication, literature is concerned with joy and creativity.

Literature covers many aspects such as metaphysics, nationality, religion, culture, society, etc. Above all, it is the aesthetic sensibility through which a work of art and literature can be appreciated. The critical appreciation of literary texts develops a sense of aesthetic judgement, linguistic ability, creative and analytical faculty, and so on. A kind of critical and aesthetic judgement the readers try to draw from the text. The readers remain busy by appreciating the text in their own way with their own sensibilities, feelings and aptitude.

Stages in Language Acquisition

Children do not wake up one morning with a fully formed grammar in their hands or with all the 'rules' of social and communicative exchanges. Linguistic knowledge develops by stages. The earliest studies of child language acquisition come from diaries kept by parents or nurses. More recent studies include tape recordings, videotapes, etc.

The stages of language acquistion can be divided into prelinguistic and linguistic stages. The earliest cries, whimpers and cooings of the new born cannot be considered early language. During this stage, the noises produced by infants in all language communities sound the same. New born infants respond to phonetic cantrasts are found in some human languages even when these differences are not phonemic in the language spoken in the baby's home.

The next stage is babbling. During this period children learn to distinguish between the sounds of their language and the sounds that are not part of the language. During the babbling period the pitch or intonation contours infants' utterances that begin to sound like adults.

In the next stage, children learn to use one-word sentences (holophrastic). For example,

"up" for   'Get me up'
"down" for   'Get down'
"daddy"   —
"light"   —

Use of holophrastic sentences marks the developing use of language for social purposes. Phonologically, children of this period prefer monosyllabic with a CV (consonant-vowel) form.

Next is the two-word stage. During the two-word period there are no syntactic or morphological markers—no inflections for number, terse, person, etc. The language of this kind seems to be a kind of pidgin. Pronounce is rare. The two words can express a number of different grammatical relations. For example.

"bat chair" for 'the bat is on the chair.'
"daddy bad" for 'my daddy is bad.'

In the next stage children produce sentences that are more closely approximate to the adult grammar. The children start stringing more than two words together. They also reveal their group of the principle of sentence formation. In this stage children learn to use inflections and other complexities in language use.

Difference between Acquisition and Learning

The term 'acquisition', when used of language, refers to the gradual development of ability in a language by using it naturally in communicative situations. The term 'learning' means a conscious process of accumulating knowledge of grammar and vocabulary of a language. In India, students learn their second language in school. They do not pick up their second language from society as they do in their first language (mother tongue). Even in ideal acquisition / learning situations, very few adults seem to reach native-like proficiency in using a second language. There are individuals who can achieve great expertise in writing skill, but not in speaking skill : 'Mother tongue pull' drags them back. One perfect example is the great Polish novelist Joseph Canrad. His novels are of great literary value. But his English speech is not free from Polish accent. Joseph Conrad syndrome is relevant in a multilingual country.

Bilingualism

A bilingual is one who speaks two languages. For a bilingual, both the language learning / acquiring experiences count. Different bilinguals have distinct uses and various levels of competence (linguistic and communicative). According to Bloomfield, bilingualism is "near-native control of two or more languages." It is the practice of "alternately using two languages" (Weinreich). Sociolinguistic and psycholinguistic parameters determine the selection of language(s) in alternative needs of people. Indians are mainly bilingual users of language(s). We have our first language, like Bangla, Hindi, Tamil, etc. English is our second language. Our society makes room for creative hybridization of languages. But what constitutes a bilingual environment? Immrigration involves leaving the country of origin in order to settle, once and for all, in a 'host' country. The children of immigrants usually acquire their first language at home from their parents and family and their second, from people outside home or school patterns. Migration is another option that generates bilingualism. Close contact with other linguistic groups in some multinational states or countries with rich linguistic diversity creates opportunities for bilingualism. Nowadays, schooling can play a very important role in making children bilingual. The education policy of states may deliberately be geared towards forstering of bilingualism. Above all, at the family level there are many different strategies to choose for bringing children up bilingually. Not all families opt, for a consistent pattern of language use; nor do they always adhere to the one-parent-one-language principle.

Skutnabb-Kangas classifies the word 'bilinguals' into four broad groups :

(a) **Elite bilingualism**
(b) **Children from linguistic majorities**
(c) **Children from bilingual families**
(d) **Children from linguistic minorities**

These four broad groups depend on four broad-based factors:
(a) The prerequisties for bilingualism.
(b) Pressure to become bilingual.
(c) The consequences entailed in failing to become bilingual.
(d) Route by which the individual has become bilingual.

In a bilingual condition, the speaker should not be considered to be of two complete (or incomplete) monolinguals. Two languages (or more languages) usually fulfil different social and linguistic roles and functions. Their distribution can be decided by a number of sociolinguistic and psycholinguistic factors. Language is always used within a cultural environment, and the context tends to vary from one speech community to another.

India is a vast and almost an endless country. Here, English and Indian languages "co-exist in a diglossic relationship" (Parasher, 1979). In India, learning English in addition to one's first language is becoming the order of the day. 'Second Language' familiarity is a matter of necessity and in a sense a matter of prestige and privilege. In most cases English coexists with state-languages of India. For example in West Bengal the state-language is 'Bangla' whereas English is used as the 'second language'. English is the state-language in the states like Mizoram and Nagaland. There are tribal languages in both of these North-eastern states. English cannot be their native language. Generally, English is used as the 'Second Language' in India. "Second Language" stands for a cover term for any language other than the 'First Language' (FL) learned /acquired by a particular or a set of learners (a) irrespective of the type of learning conditions and (b) irrespective of the number of the other non-native languages possessed by the learners. 'Second Language' is abbreviated to L2 (where as the 'first language' is abbreviated to L1). An L2, then, means, unless specified, a particular 'non-native language under discussion', that is so called 'Target Language' (TL). In the linguistically and culturally pluralistic Indian subcontinent English is used as the 'Second Language' which is acquired after one has learnt the First Language.

The teaching of English in India involves a complex network of activities. It involves the political decision makers who take broad-based decisions, the Boards / Universities who frame the course, design the syllabus; who appoint teachers and administrative (academic) chairs and who frame a module for evaluation and other rules and regulation regarding teaching as well as learning and at last, the classroom teachers—the link between the entire

English teaching programme and the target learners. The entire scheme of teaching of English in India can be shown in the following Pyramid:

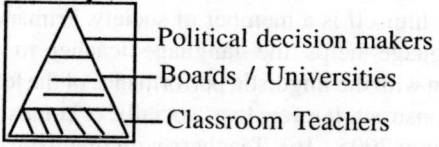
- Political decision makers
- Boards / Universities
- Classroom Teachers

Learning of English in India continues to be governed by both academic consideration and socio-political considerations. And we have an atmosphere in which we plead for the continuance of teaching English on the basis of following factors:

1. English is a 'window on the world'. It is an established international link language.
2. English is the 'library language'. A large number of periodicals, journals and resource books are written in English.
3. We need English for residing abroad.
4. It is the language of international trade.
5. Indian English is a sociolinguistic reality today. Indian writing in English has earned world-wide recognition.
6. English is necessary for specialised jobs like interpretation, broadcasting, translation, etc.
7. English serves as a link and shared language among the educated Indians.
8. English is the language of intelligentia.

Relevance of Linguistics to Language Teaching

Language teaching is multi-dimensional and interdisciplinary activity. It is a process by which a teacher teaches a language in a classroom or in similar situation. The teacher in the language teaching / learning situation is aware of the objective of language teaching and brings to bear deductive and analytical abilities to teach the language effectively. A teacher exploits a wide range of strategies to enable the learners to learn the language successfully.

Linguistics is the scientific study of language. The job of a linguist is to construct theory analysing linguistic data and to predict the potential data. Applied linguistics is concerned with the identification and analysis of a certain class of problems which arise in the setting up and carrying out of language teaching programmes. A language teacher is destined to teach his students how to use language. If he gets an insight into the mechanism of the language that he is teaching, he can perform his role as a language teacher successfully. He is sure to show better performance than one who does not know the mechanism of language.

Linguistic study of language is one of the resources of a total language teaching activity. It is an obvious impetus for the language teachers, course designers, and producers of teaching materials. It is a socio-individual event. The language user himself is a member of society. Primary knowledge of the sociology of language helps the language teacher to predict the social variables in relation with the linguistic performance of the learners. 'Register' is a sociolinguistic construct. It refers to a "socially, or contextually, defined style of language" (Sarangi 2005 : 16). Teachers with linguistic exposure can map / plot the specific linguistic usage of any individual within a social group. The dimensions of variability in language have been related to social characteristics of the learner.

Socio-pragmatics is a recent development to study 'discourse'. Discourse is an organised speech process. It is a mechanism by which communication is maintained. The main objective of teaching / learning a language is to develop the skills of communication through that channel. Knowledge of sociolinguistics helps the teacher to understand the appropriacy and the acceptability of language in a discourse (as used by the learners). The factors that go into the successful participation in a linguistic exchange are :
(a) Sender
(b) Receiver
(c) Code
(d) Channel
(e) Situation / Context

Language is the outcome of the interaction between an innate structure of human mind and socio-cultural objective reality. Psycholinguistics in the study of the mental process underlying the planning, production, transmission, perception and comprehension of speech activity. It is closely related to clinical linguistics and aphysiology. Psycholinguistics helps the language teacher to identify different psychology related issues which go into the linguistic output. It also concerns with human brain and the neurons. Knowledge of psycholinguistics is a must to predict the stages of language acquisition. Critical studies have proved that language learning skills are mainly psycholinguistic guess works.

It has been accepted by all interested in the education that error is inevitable in the process of learning. A learner errors provide evidence of the system of the language that he is using at a particular point in the course. These errors provide evidence of how language is acquired. What strategies the learner is employing in has language learning process. Linguistics do not dictate any methodology to language teachers. But, teachers who know Linguistics can make use of error analysis to find out the causes of these developmental errors and to take necessary measures to avoid them. Similarly, a language teacher with knowledge of linguistics may be able to correct to pronunciation of the learner who carries the strong influence of his first language (L_1) on the pronunciation of his target language. After sufficient training in phonetic notation and vocal sounds, a learner finds humself fully equipped to utter speech sounds. Accent or stress plays important role in some languages like English. Knowledge of Phonetics can help the language teacher to use acceptable and mutually intelligible accent in the language class.

A language teacher can never ignore the teaching of grammar. At times, selection of a grammar book creates doubt in the mind of language teacher. A grammar book is supposed to be the blueprint of the grammar syllabus. A teacher who knows linguistics should not find difficulty in selecting the right kind of grammar book. According to H.E. Palmer (1971 : 173), gradation means passing from the known to the unknown by easy stages, each of which serves as preparation for the next. Knowledge in Linguistics may come in selecting a properly graded, grammar book and offer linguistically graded phonological, syntactical and lexical patterns.

Linguistic insights can be used to organize the different facets of language teaching such as syllabus-framing, teaching of grammar, composition, spelling, reading, listening and pronunciation of speech sounds. "Our understanding of Linguistics ('Semantics' in particular) can help us to meet the problems of translation effectively. In the post-colonial period the resistance of the dominated language-culture to neo-colonial linguistic-cultural hegemony, is at times, quite vivid" (Ramakrishna 1997 : 31), Translation is one of the ways of reconciling the interests of different groups. It is one of the areas studied by linguists and translators. Knowledge of translation (a linguistic activity) helps a language teacher to teach in mixed multilingual classrooms of India.

Distance education is becoming the order of the day. Instructional objectives must, therefore, be achieved by efficiency methods rather than through personal interaction. At present, the role of the classroom teacher is under tremendous threat. Books have appeared with such titles as 'Goodbye Teacher!' (Keller 1968 : 79-89) Teachers are going to be replaced by "the new media and by learning package" (Maddox 1988 : 286). Linguists will have to play a significant role to design new types of objective-specific courses.

TWO GREAT ORISSAN PILGRIMS: A SOCIOLINGUISTIC STUDY

Bibhu Padhi and Niranjan Mohanty, two Orissan poetic pilgrims, do not belong to the so-called hubs of literary administration, politics and favouritism. They are not metro-bred; they grew up listening to the incessant pitter-patter of raindrops, the silent cry of common birds and animals. The poet in Mohanty identifies himself with rain. In the absence of rain, he makes a house of rains and under its roof, he sits in order to listen to the sound of "rain-drops falling all night." Padhi's 'Rains in Cuttack' is a poetic rapture of rain's whisper; the poet seeks permission from his mother to make the mudgreen carpet his own. For Padhi, the adults always disturb him and hence, he feels that he is "still a child somewhere". Both the poets love dragging their wings beyond the demon of sound; exploring the water songs. Both of them belong to the land of Jagannatha; a rich socio-cultural and religious heritage which speaks through their poetic lines. The Orissan landscape has a mysterious charm to turn man to look into the inscape and feel the bond with the greater humanity. Some of the Orissan poets have embraced English to spread the native fragrance. Jayanta Mahapatra holds the distinction of being the first Indian English poet to have received the Sahitya Akademi Award (1981) for *Relationship*. He started writing poetry at the age of thirty-eight, quite late in normal standard. And immediately his poetry received accolades from knowledgeable quarters. Rooted in mythical-historical past of Orissa, and yet not unaware of the sociological changes in the contemporary society, he beautifully recreates in the mode of his poetic expression the landscape and people around him. In his poetry, Mahapatra sings of the hearts and minds of many things of nature, on the basis of his sincere love for all creation. Poverty, deprivation, social injustice, the plight of the Indian woman and prostitute recur in his verses. His poem, "Dawn at Puri", the most sacred place in the myths and history of Orissa. The poem has the glow and charm of some Metaphysical conceits and images. The very beginning opens with the images of a "skull":

"Endless crow noises
A skull on the holy sands
Tilts its empty country towards hunger"

Mahapatra's influence on contemporary Oriya poets (writing in English) like Bibhu Padhi, Niranjan Mohanty, Prabhanjan Mishra and Rabindra K. Swain is worth mentioning. Jayanta Mahapatra has also inspired (directly/indirectly) the diasporic Indian English poets like Meena Alexander and Shanta Acharya for their career in poetry. Both Bibhu Padhi and Niranjan Mohanty share intimate bonds with Mahapatra family. Both of them have contributed extensively to the *Chandrabhaga*, the magazine run by Jayanta Mahapatra.

Padhi and Mohanty have been writing poetry out of their silence, 'far from the madding crowd's ignoble strife'. Bibhu Padhi, the poet of our inner (pre-speech) world, constructs the poetics of silence in many of his poems. His poetry is the redolent of the Orissa scene. His 'Konarake' is poem of thinking aloud—"The dark fate lies hard/ upon stones that never speak." The ruin state of the Sun Temple at Konaraka casts 'sad ancient shadows'. Its glorious past speaks through the majestic silence imprinted in the texture of its body:

> I smell its loneliness—insistent and tender
> Like the love that it holds, far within.

Konaraka 'connects our desire/with the open sky.' The 'desiring stones' echo the solitude from the pauses of decay and death. Shadows of nostalgic past linger as time marches ahead.

Niranjan Mohanty in his poem, 'A Tiger Always Lifts Me To A Garden'writes:

> "The garden only matters
> For my floating into its lair
> Transforms me into a garden."

The 'Tiger', beyond its collective cruelty, takes man to the silent zones of the anecdotes of roots and lullabies. The muse sings in the poet as he opens the eternal pages of silence. In the 'Epilogue'of *Krishna* Mohanty writes, "I sculpted my loneliness /on the sleek back of darkness." Mohanty is a poet of 'blue whispers of hearts, immaculate'.

The poet's heart is a forest which is burnt with 'wild fires of fears and grief'; the jottings of a 'throbbing heart' reflects the inscription on a 'flaming blood'. Like a devotional poet Mohanty longs for Lord's 'umbrella', signifying love and grace, when it rains and in the hour of hard times. For the poet, prayer is the only means to reach Him and hence for him "Every moment / is a moment of prayer and prayer".

A beguiling sense of trauma of living, alienation under the alien sky and the paradoxical overlapping of time and space pervade Padhi's poems which probably spring from his own private (may be mental) agony. Indeed, each poem in *Going to the Temple* to *Stories of the Night* is rich with varied dexterity. His poems are subtle and elusive that explore the states of mind and genuine sentiments. Padhi explores the tantalising gap between the space he writes from and the world outside:

> You are the exiled one.
> No one listens to your words.

There is a straddling of public and private spheres; an indomitable gusto of intensity marks Padhi's poetic lines. His 'Terraced Lines' reminds us 'pattern poetry':

Which land?
What flat lands?
What flat lands are these?
What seeds are you sowing
on your horizontal bed, brother?
What childlike plants shall grow here?
Who shall take care of them with the love
they will need so dearly for so long until they can
stand on their own, look back and smile for having received
the love they needed at the right time of growing up into themselves?

Who shall be
with them, brother?
Who shall watch them play
against the breeze, frolickingly?
Who shall wait for their simple falls,
the undertermined fate of their catching
a fever or cold, breathing without breath for life?
Who shall be around them to tell them that nothing
is to be feared, nothing lost by a fever or a cold, once it was
decided that they would be reared up with all the care they'd ever need?

Tender souls
that chose to descend
to the flat horizontals for
an honest, hard, vertical life.
They'd be with us for a while,
a season only, and then shall precede
all our loves and sympathies, in spite of our
very human efforts, our cries and bewilderments.
Will you be there to watch their going away to where they
came from, much without our efforts, so much without ourselves.

Can you bear
the grief of seasonal loss?
Your face tells me, you do not
have the strength, the sheer physical
strength to do that, and therefore cannot,
without at the same time losing a considerable part
of yourself, your land—flat lands—your fingers, your ancestors.
What are you going to do then? Who shall listen to what you say?

Who shall understand your recent loss, your bright, magnificent loss?
And hence, I am here, all through, to share your happiness and loss.

On the other hand, Mohanty's poetic mode ranges from the meditative to sensuous where the metaphysical subtlety of arrivals and departures get confused. A feature that impresses and ultimately convinces the readers is the poets' readiness to allow conflicting voices to be heard from all contending perspectives. He gives an outlet to the pain through words but remains allusive and suggestive.

> "Sometimes, like pain, something spreads
> within. I'm not clear in what I write.
> I fail to grasp the meaning of what I chisel."

Poems of Padhi and Mohanty pose a tension that reaches out to the reader, arousing in one a sense of need that can not be satisfied. The use of private symbols and seemingly opaque images demand a thorough and close reading of their poems. They are rooted in Orrisan landscape which needs no declaration, no proclamation and no assertion. The authenticity in the relationship between land and identity that the poems of Padhi and Mohanty bear is a matter to be felt and realised. Jayanta Mahapatra honestly proclaimed:

> To Orissa, to this land in which my roots lie and lies my past and in which lies my beginning and my end, where the wind keens over the grip of the River Daya and where the waves of the bay of Bengal fail to reach out today to the twilight soul of Konark, I acknowledge my relationship. (*The Golden Voices*, ii)

Poems of Bibhu Padhi and Niranjan Mohanty have both the feeling and the form blended together. At times their poems appear anomalous, arbitrary and very much tentative, but they show and suggest the flux that enlivens life, mortality and poetic aesthetics. The poets find themselves vacillating between the duality of their inevitable cultural and traditional roots on one hand and their predominantly training in English literary tradition on the other. As a result, their individual poetic persona is faced with a unique and irresolvable dilemma, between two opposing value systems generated by these two paradoxical positions. The phrases and expressions of both the poets are sincerely poetic that transforms the readers from sadness to joy; charmingly integrated and suggestive, and the treatment is modernistic. They remind us of modern poetic style mostly found in the poetry of T.S. Eliot, W. B. Yeats, Walter de la Mare and W.H. Auden.

BIBLIOGRAPHY

Adams, U.	*An Introduction to Modern Word formation.* London: Longman, 1973.
Barthes, R.	*Critical Essays* trans. Howard. Illionoi, 1972.
Bloomfield, L.	*Language* New York : Rinehart, 1933.
Cardona.G.	*Panini: A survey of Research.* New Delhi: MBD, 1980.
Chomsky, N.	*Language and Mind* ed. Harcourt Brace, New York 1972.
	Reflections on Language, New York: Partheon Books, 1975.
Das, M.	*"Teaching English Literature"* Replica. Vol.VI,II, 2003, 41.
De Renzi, E.	A. Pieczuro, and L.Vignolo. 1966. *Oral apraxia and aphasia. Cactex* 2, 50-73.
Homes, J.	*An Introduction to Sociolinguistic,* London: Longman. 1992.
Hymes, Dell	*Foundations of Sociolinguistics,* Pennysylvania: P.U. Press, 1974.
Iyergar, K.R.S.	*Indian Writing in English,* New Delhi: Starling, 1984, 63-64.
Keller.F.	'Goodbye Teacher' *Journal of Applied Behaviour Analysis.* 1968. 79-89.
Maddox. H	*How to Study* Calcutta: Rupa and Co. 1988 (1st Pub. 1963). 286.
Mukherjee, Meenakshi.	*The Twice Born Fiction.* Arnold Heinemann Publisher, 1974.
Palmer. H.E.	'Grading I' *Language Teaching Texts,* London: OUP, 1971.
Parasher, S.V.	*Indian English : Certain Grammatical and Stylistic Features.* World Guide. 1983.
Prabhu, N.S.	*Second Language Pedagogy,* "JALT Journal" 21(I), 1987, 125-142.
Ramakrishna. S. (Ed.)	*Translation and Multiculturalism.* New Delhi: Pencraft International, 1997, 31.
Sarangi, J.	*Indian Novels in English : A Sociolinguistic Study.* Prakash Book Depat : Bareilly, 2005.
Sebeak. T.A. (e.d),	*Style in Language*: MIT Press, 1961.
Trudgill, P.	*The Dialects of England.* London : Blackwell, 1990.
Verma, S.K. and Krishnaswami, N.	*Modern Linguistics,* Delhi : OUP, 1989.
Williams, G.	*Sociolinguistics.* London : Routledge, 1992.
Wright, L. and Hope, J.	*Stylistics.* London. Routledge, 1995.
Yalden, J.	*Principles of Course Design:* CUP, 1987-88.
Young, D.J.	*Introduction to English Grammar,* London: Routledge, 1984.

"There're quite a few things to be crossed over so that you may reach the farther shore."

'Crossing Over': Bibhu Padhi

Part II : Phonetics

Part II : Phonetics

PHONETICS & ORGANS OF SPEECH

Linguistics is a scientific study of language. Phonetics is a branch of Linguistics, which deals with production, transmission and reception of speech sounds. Thus, the study of speech sound is known as Phonetics. Phonetics is concerned with how speech sounds are produced in the vocal tract and the physical propertice of it. It is made at three different stages : (a) *Articulatory Phonetics* (which deals with the production of speech), (b) *Acoustic Phonetics* (which deals with the transmission of speech throught air). This is concerned with studying the properties of sound as a consequence of vibrations in air pressure and (c) *Auditory Phonetics* (which deals with the reception of speech sounds by the internal diaphragm fitted in the ear-cavity.) The outer ear collects the sound, the middle ear amplifies them and passes them to the inner are. The sounds are smeared across each other.

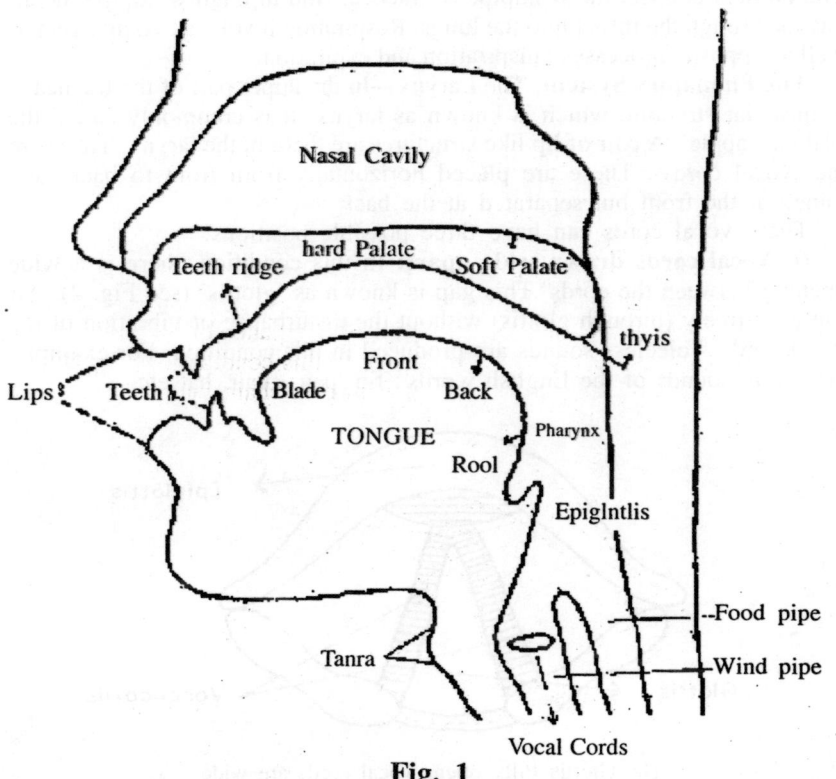

Fig. 1

Organs of Speech: Actually, speech is 'modulated breathing'. Air streams make speech sounds possible. The air (mainly lung-air) that flows out of the mouth gets modulated into speech sounds with the help of certain organs of the body. These organs are referred to as organs of speech. The organs of speech can be divided into three heads :

(a) The Respiratory System: This system involves the lungs, the chest muscles and the trachea or the windpipe.

(b) The Phonatory system: This system involves the larynx (the upper part of the trachea).

(c) The Articulatory System: This system comprises the pharynx (the cavity forming the upper part of the gullet), the teeth, tongue, the roof of the mouth, the lips and the nose.

The Respiratory System: This system consists of the lungs, the muscles of the chest and trachea or windpipe. The lungs are spongy bodies. They are made up of alveoli (small spongy sacs). Small tubes that supply air to these alveoli are bronchioles. The large unified bronchioles are known as bronchi. The bronchi connect the windpipe or trachea. And through windpipe the air passes through the throat into the lungs. Respiration involves two different as well as opposite processes : inspiration and expiration.

The Phonatory System: The Larynx—In the upper part of the trachea is a muscular structure which is known as larynx. It is commonly called the 'Adam's apple'. A pair of lip like structures are there in the larynx. These are the 'vocal cords'. These are placed horizontally from front to back, and joined at the front but separated at the back.

These vocal cords can have three possible positions.

(i) **Vocal cords drawn wide apart:** In this condition, there is a wide opening between the cords. This gap is known as 'glottis' (see Fig. 2). Air can pass freely (through glottis) without the disturbance or vibration of the vocal cords. Voiceless sounds are produced in this condition. For example, the initial sounds of the English words : tin, pen, chair, hat etc.

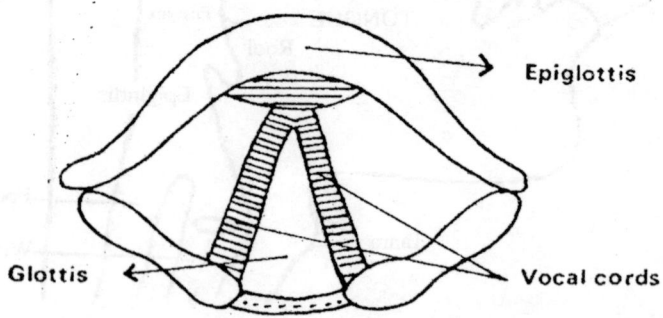

The Glottis fully open. Vocal cords are wide
Fig. 2

(ii) **Vocal cords held loosely together:** In this structure of the vocal cords vibration is a must. Generally voiced sounds are produced under such condition. For example, the initial sounds in English words: bat, got, nun, must, etc.

(iii) **Vocal cords held together (tightly):** In this structure, the glottis remains closed. Air cannot pass through the glottis. Vocal cords stand in this condition at the time of eating and drinking.

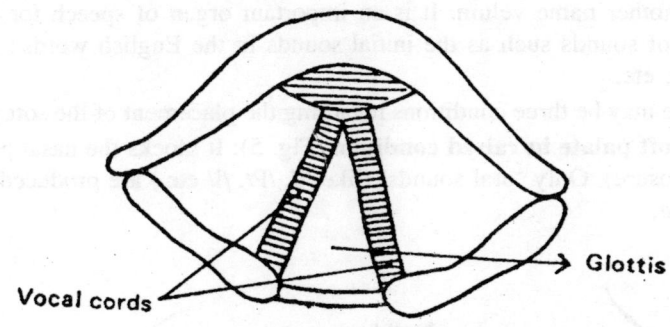

Fig. 3
Vocal cords wide and the glottis fully open-position for breath and during the production of voiceless sounds.

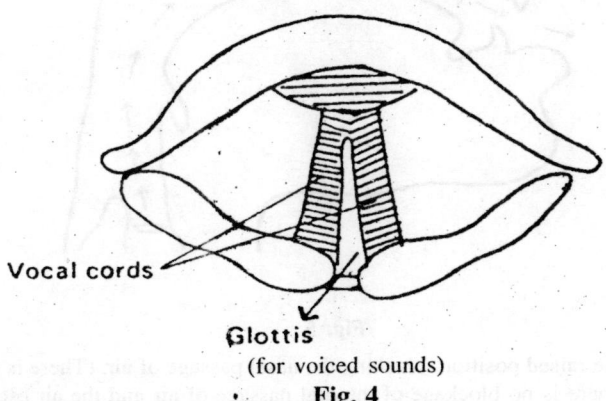

(for voiced sounds)
Fig. 4

Articulatory System

The lips : The lips play crucial role in the production of speech sounds. The initial sounds in the English words pin and bill, bag, for example, are made with the help of lips. The lips play an important part even in producing some vowel sounds (as in the initial sound of wet) in English.

The teeth: Some English consonants are produced with the help of teeth. For example, the initial sounds of father, this, than etc.

The tongue: It is an important organ of speech. Tongue is divided into three distinct parts—tip, blade and front. It is flexible by nature. The tongue is moved accordingly to produce English speech sounds.

The hard and soft palate: The hard palate is the bony, concave surface lying immediately behind teeth ridge.

The soft portion of the roof after the hard palate is known as soft palate. It has another name velum. It is an important organ of speech for a large number of sounds such as the initial sounds in the English words : knight, gain, go, etc.

There may be three conditions regarding the placement of the soft palate :

(a) **Soft palate in raised condition** (Fig. 5): It blocks the nasal passage. (velic closure). Only 'oral sounds' (like /t/, /P/, /l/ etc.) are produced in this condition.

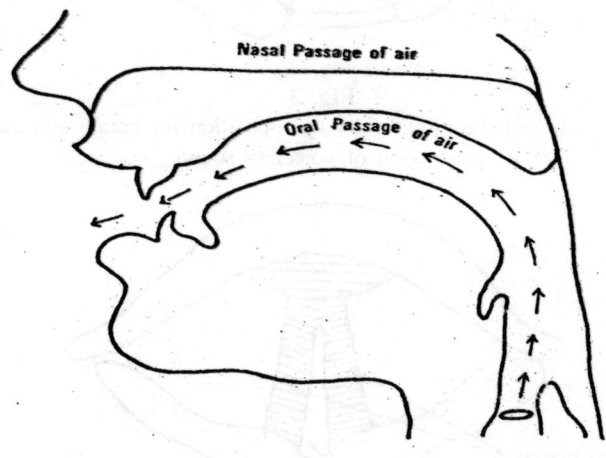

Fig. 5

Velum in the raised position, blocking the nasal passage of air. (There is *velic closure*). There is no blockage of the oral passage of air and the air escapes though the mouth (indicated by arrows). *Production of oral sounds.*

(b) **Soft palate is lowered :** There is no velic closure. It is velic opening. The oral passage is blocked by closing the lips. Air can escape only through the nose (Fig. 6). Nasal Sounds (like /m/n/y) are produced in this conditions.

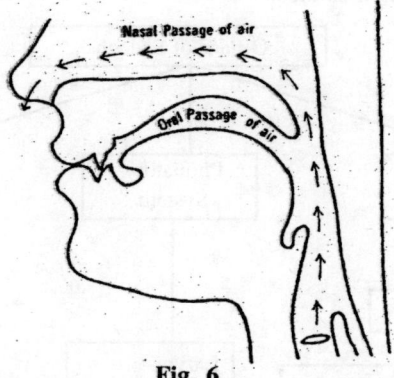

Fig. 6

Velum lowered. (There is *no* velic closure ; there is a velic opening.) The oral passage is blocked (in this case) by closing the lips. The air from the lungs escapes through the nose (indicated by arrows). **Production of a nasal sound.**

(c) **Soft palate is lowered, but there is no blockage at the oral or nasal passage :** In this condition (see Fig. 7) there is neither velic or oral closure. Nasalised sounds are produced in this condition. (i) The last sound in the French word 'bon' (good) is an example of nasalised sound. (ii) The vowel sound in the *Bangla* word, 'বাঁশ' Bansh (bamboo) is a nasalized sound.

This sound has the symbol (~) at the top of the respective sound.

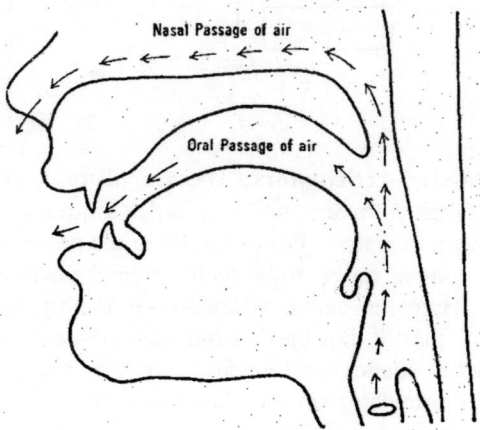

Fig. 7

The soft palate is lowered, thus opening the nasal passage of air. There is no blockage of the oral passage of air. The air escapes simultaneously through the nose and the mouth (indicated by arrows). There is neither velic closure nor any oral closure.

Production of nasalised sounds.

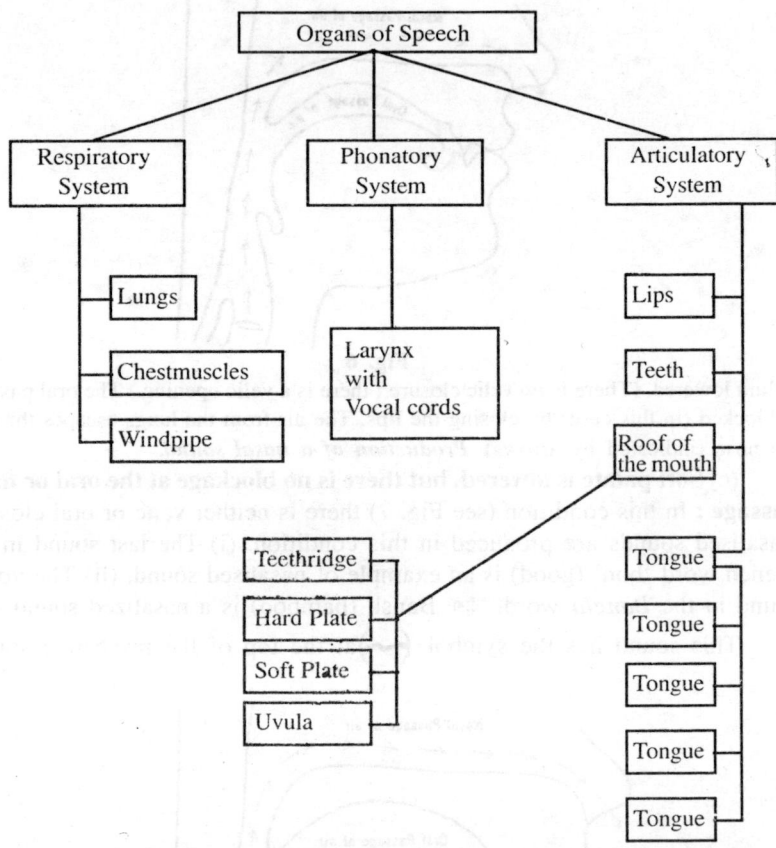

Active and Passive Articulators: The articulators (organs of speech) which move from their normal position in order to produce speech sounds are knwon as active articulators. For example: in the production of |t| the tip and blade of the tongue move from their original positions to articulate against the teeth. Here the active articulator is the tip and blade of the tongue. The organs that do not move from their position in the process of productions of speech sounds are knwon as passive articulators. Teethridge acts as the passive articulator (in the above example).

The Air-Stream Mechanisms: Lung air is used in the process of articulation of most speech sounds of most language. An air-stream is produced in air-stream mechanism. It has close approximity with the behaviour of a flitgun. There are three kinds of air-stream mechanisms involved in the articulation of speech sounds (in English):

Phonetics & Organs of Speech

(a) **Pulmonic air-stream mechanism :** The walls of the lungs act as the initiator. It is the most important air-stream mechanism for the production of speech sounds.
(b) **Glottalic air-stream mechanism :** The closed glottis acts as the initiator. The air in the phraynx is used in the process.
(c) **Velaric air-stream mechanism :** For this mechanism the back of the tongue is the initiator and the air in the mouth is used in the process.

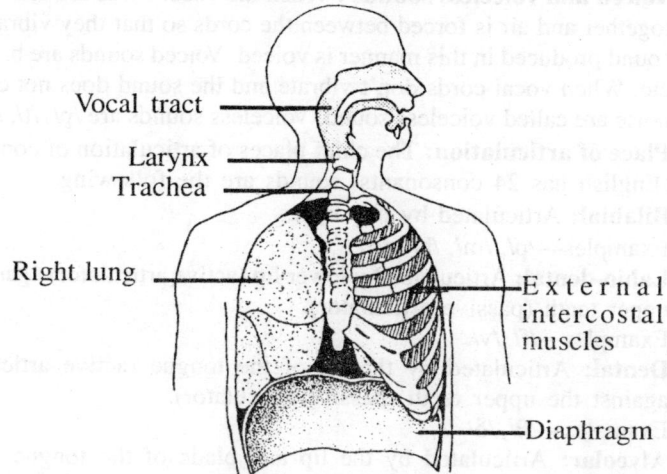

Major anatomical structures involve in the production of speech (Fig. 8).

When the air-stream mechanism is used to push air out, it is known as 'egressive' and when it is used to take air in, it is called 'ingressive'. We use 'pulmonic egressive air-stream mechanism' for the production of the sounds in English and 'pulmonic ingressive air-stream mechanism' for yawning and snoring, but obviously not for speaking.

EXERCISE

1. What is air-stream mechanism? How many types of air-stream mechanisms are there?
2. What are the organs responsible for speech? Draw the organs of speech. What is respiratory system? What are the organs related to this system?
3. Describe the Phonetic function of the following organs of speech :
   (a) Vocal cords
   (b) Soft palate
   (c) The tongue
   (d) Teeth
   (e) Lips

CLASSIFICATION OF SOUNDS

The traditional phonetic classification of speech sounds is based on three variables :
- (a) In terms of voiced and voiceless sounds—
- (b) Place of articulation—
- (c) Manner of articulation—
- (a) **Voiced and voiceless sounds :** When the vocal cords are drawn near together and air is forced between the cords so that they vibrate, the sound produced in this manner is voiced. Voiced sounds are b, d, g, i, etc. When vocal cords don't vibrate and the sound does not contain noise are called voiceless sound. Voiceless sounds are /p/, /t/, /k/ etc.
- (b) **Place of articulation:** The chief places of articulation of consonant (English has 24 consonants) sounds are the following :
  - (i) **Bilabial:** Articulated by two lips.
    Examples—/p/, /m/, /b/ etc.
  - (ii) **Labio-dental:** Articulated by lower lip (active articulator) against the upper teeth (passive articulator).
    Examples—/f/, /v/.
  - (iii) **Dental:** Articulated by the tip of the tongue (active articulator) against the upper teeth (passive articulator).
    Examples—/θ/, /ð/
  - (iv) **Alveolar:** Articulated by the tip and blade of the tongue (active articulator) against the teethridge (passive articulator).
    Example—/t/, /d/.
  - (v) **Post-alvelor:** Articulated by the tip of the tongue (active articulator) against the backpart of teethridge (passive articulator).
    Example—/r/.
  - (vi) **Palato-alveolar:** Articulated by the blade or front of the tongue (active articulator) against the teeth-ridge or hard palate (passive articulator).
    Exmpale—The initial sounds English words 'chair', 'jail' and 'shame'.
  - (vii) **Palatal:** Articulated by the front of the tongue (a.a) against the hard palate (p.a.).
    Example—The initial sound in the English word 'yes'.
    [a.a. is active articulator and p.a. is passive articulator]
  - (viii) **Velar :** Articulated by the back of the tongue (a.a.) against the soft plage (p.a.)
    Example—/k/.
  - (ix) **Glottal:** Articulated in the glottis. Two vocal cords are the articulators.
    Example—The initial sound in the English word 'hen'.

Classification of Sounds 149

A part from these nine categories we farther have 'retroflex' and 'uvular'. English has no retroflex or uvular sounds. Hindi has retroflex sounds. Hindi has no uvular sound.

Liquids: Liquid sounds are found in the overwhelming majority of the world's languages. English has two voiced ones: |l| and |r|. The term liquid is an impressionistic expression indicating that the sound is 'smooth' and 'flows easily'. Liquids share properties of both consonants and vowels : as in the articulation of certain consonants, the tongue (blade of it) is raised toward the alveolar ridge; as in the articulation of vowels, air is allowed to pass through the oral cavity without great friction.

|l| is a lateral alveolar liquid.

|r| is a nonlateral alveolar liquid.

(c) **Manner of articulation:** It specifies the kind of closure or narrowing or release involved in the production of sounds.

If we analyse the consonants according to the manner in which the organs of speech articulate them, we can divide them in the following classes :

(i) **Plosive:** The process involved is the complete closure and sudden release. It makes an explosive sound. There are three phases in the production of plosive consonants.

    (a) The closure phase.
    (b) The closed phase.
    (c) The release phase.

Example—The initial sounds in the English words—pen, ten, den etc.

(ii) **Affricate:** The process involved is the complete closure and slow release.

Example—The initial sounds in the English words : chair and church.

(iii) **Nasal:** Formed by complete closure of mouth. The air has free pass through the nose. The process is complete oral closure.

Example—The final sounds in the English words : ran, sing, etc.

(iv) **Lateral:** The process involved is partial closure. Formed by an obstacle in the middle of the mouth, the air can be released through both sides of the obstacle.

Example—The initial sound of the English word : love.

(v) **Fricatives:** The manner involved is close approximation. The lung-air escapes through the narrow space between the active and passive articulators, producting audible friction.
Example—The initial sounds in the English words : then, sheep, fat etc.

(vi) **Rolled:** Formed by rapid succession of 'taps' on some elastic organ.
Example—The initial sound in the English word : 'red'.

(vii) **Flapped:** Formed by a single 'tap'.
Example—r sound in very (by some English people).
In this case the active articulator strikes against the passive articulator just once and then quickly flaps forward.

(viii) **Frictionless continuant:** Sounds produced in this manner should not be accompanied by audible friction. The stricture involved is—open approximation.
Example—The common r-sound in RP (Received Pronunciation)

(ix) **Semi-vowel:** Semi-vowels are vowels but function as consonants. The stricture involved is—open approximation.
Example—The initial sounds of the English words : yes, wet, etc.
[Sounds articulated with a stricture of open approximation are known as approximants.]

The above classification can be put into a tabular form:

CLASSIFICATION OF SOUNDS

Place→ Manner ↓	Bilabial	Labio-dental	Dental	Alveolar	Post-Alveolar	Palato-Alveolar	Palatal	Velar	Glottal
Nasal	m			n				n	
Plosive	pb			td				kg	
Affricate						tʃ dz			
Fricative		fv	θ ð	sz		ʃ z			h
Lateral				l					
Approximants	w				r		j	(w)	

English consonants are 24 in number. Six of them are plosives, two affricates, three nasals, nine fricatives, one lateral and three approximants.

There are broad-based classes of sounds—consonants and vowels. Vowels are articulated with a stricture of open approximation.

Classification of Sounds

English has twelve 'pure vowels' and eight diphthongs. Pure vowels consist of single vowel sound. Vowels that change their quality are called diphthongs. And vowels that do not change their quality are called pure vowels or monophthongs.

Pure Vowels & Their Phonetic Symbols

1. / i : /   as in 'beat', 'seen'
2. / I /   as in 'bit', 'hit'
3. / e /   as in 'ten', 'lend'
4. / æ /   as in 'sat', 'and'
5. / a : /   as in 'cart', 'car'
6. / ɐ/   as in 'cot'
7. / ɔ: /   as in 'caught'
8. / ʊ /   as in 'full'
9. / u : /   as in 'fool'
10. / ʌ/   as in 'bus'
11. / ɜ: /   as in 'shirt'
12. / ə/   as in 'china' [final]
    as in 'ago' [non-final]

of these 12 pure vowels (a) four are front vowels : / i :, I, e, æ /, (b) five back vowels : a:, a, c:, u, u: / and (c) three central vowels : v/, 3:, e/. These vowels are placed in figures below :

English diphthongs are :
1. /eI/   as in 'day', 'tail'
2. /aI/   as in 'tile'
3. /ɔI/   as in 'foil'
4. /eu/   as in 'go'
5. /au/   as in 'cow'
6. /Iə/   as in 'tear'
7. /e /   as in 'fair'
8. /u /   as in 'poor'

Diacritic : It is a symbol that indicates the pronunciation value of a speech item (segment). Diacritics are not pronounced themselves but supply information about pronunciation. The voiced phonemes like |b|, |d|, |g|, lose their voicing at the ends of words. This can be shown by diacritics. For example, $\begin{bmatrix} t \\ n \end{bmatrix}$ refers to dental pronunciation of | t |.

Coronal : In articulating a [+ Coronal] phoneme, the blade of the tongue is raised toward or touches the teeth or the alveolar ridge. Dental, alveolar, and alveo-palatal consonants are [+ Coronal] phonemes.

Anterior : Anterior sounds are made with the primary constriction in front of the alveo-palatal position. Labial, dental, interdental, and alveolar articulations are [+Anterior] phonemes.

EXERCISE

1. What do you mean by voiced and voiceless sounds?
2. What are the places of articulation?
3. What are the manners of articulation?
4. What is the difference between pure vowels and diphthongs?
5. How many types of vowels are there?
6. How many diphthongs are there in English?
7. How many front vowels are there in English?
8. How many back vowels are there in English?

DESCRIPTION OF CONSONANTS, VOWELS & DIPHTHONGS

CONSONANTS

Plosive Consonants

English has six plosive consonant phonemes (the smallest unit at the level of sound) :
pb td kg
Three-term description of the plosive consonants (of English)—
/ p /— Voiceless bilabial plosive consonant
Examples : pill, pipe.
/ b /— Voiced bilabial plosive.
Examples : bad, baby.
/ t /— Voiceless alveolar plosive.
Example : tear, tin.
/ d /— Voiced alveolar plosive.
Examples : dream, dead.
/ g /— Voiced velar plosive.
Examples : god, gun.
/ k /— Voiceless velar plosive.
Example : know, knee.

Three-term Description of English Affricate Consonants

In English there are only two affricate consonant phonemes : / tʃ / dʒ /
/ tʃ /— Voiceless palato-alveolar affricate
Examples : church, charm.
/ dʒ /— Voiced palato—alveolar affricate
Examples : judge, gin.

Three-term Description of English Nasal Consonants

There are three nasal consonant phonemes in English : /m/, /n/ and /ŋ/
/m/— Voiced bilabial nasal consonant.
Examples : mat, man.
/n/— Voiced alveolar nasal consonant
Examples : not, noon.
Both /m/ and /n/ can be syllabic (as in Bottom and ridden respectively).
/ŋ/— Voiced velar nasal consonant.
Example : sing, king.

Three-term Description of English Lateral Consonant—English has only one lateral consonant phoneme : / l /
/l/— Voiced alveolar lateral consonant.

There are many allophonic (different realisations of the some phoneme) varieties of /l/. Among them *'dark/l/'* and *'clear/l/'* are most important. (l/ is 'dark' or velarized when it occurs at the word-final position or when it is followed by a consonant.

for example :

ball
tall } word-final (l) (— #). # means word boundary.
call

Cold
Milk } /l/ is followed by a consonant, (—consonant).
pulled

/l/ is 'clear' or palatalized when it is followed by a vowel or /j/ (semi-vowel).

Example :   lip
let   /l/ is followed by a vowel (—vowel).
lad
lame
allure   /l/ is followed by /j/ (—/j/).
lure

/l/ becomes syllabic in (English) words such as settle, kettle etc.

Three-term Discription of English Fricative Consonants

English has nine fricative consonant phonemes.

/f/   /s/
/v/   /z/ /h/
/θ/   /ʃ/
/ð/   /ʒ/

/f/— Voiceless labiodental fricative consonant.
Example : father, fat etc.
/v/— Voiced labiodental fricative
Example : vice, van etc.
/θ/— Voiceless dental fricative
Examples : thin, bath etc.
/ð/— Voiced dental fricative
Examples : that, booth etc.
/s/— Voiceless alveolar fricative
Examples : see, fast etc.

Pronounciation of the Suffixes—(e) s, s

(i) /z/ after a voiced sound other than /z, 3, d₃/ : girls stand.
(ii) /iz/ after /s, /z, f, 3, ff, d₃/ : roses, budges.

Description of Consonants, Vowels & Diphthongs 155

    (iii) /s/ after a voiceless sound (except)s, f, tʃ/d : cloths, stops.

/z/—   Voiced alveolar fricative.
        Examples : buzz, bags.

/ʃ/—   Voiceless palats-alveloar fricative
        Examples : ration, sure etc.

/h/—   Voiceless glottal fricative
        Examples : hat, who, etc.

Three-term Description of English Frictionless Continuants

English has only one frictionless continuant :
$$/r/$$

/r/—   Voiced post alveolar frictionless continuant.
        Examples : rude, sorry, etc.

    r—Sound is not used before consonants or word finally, unless the word is followed (immediately) by another, beginning with a vowel.
    Examples : curl (k3 : 1), there (hi) etc.

    Linking r : When a word ends with the letter r and the next word begins with a vowel and if there is no pause between the two words (within the same sense group) the final or of the first word is pronounced. This is called linking r.

    Examples :   (i) father and mother fað r nm ∂
                       (ii) far away /fa:r ewei/ ∂I aidI r vIt

    Intrusive r : An intrusive r is frequently used by analogy. Actually there is no r in spelling. When one word ends in a vowel and the next word begin with a vowel, an /r/ introduces between the two sounds.

    Example :   (i) The idea(r) of it ∂IaIdI r vIt
                    (ii) The law(r) and order.

Three Term Description of English Semi-Vowels

English has to semi-vowels.
$$/w/ \text{ and } /j/$$

(w)—voiced labio-velar semi-vowel.
Examples : west, when etc.

/j/—Voiced palatal semi-vowel
Examples : yet, suit etc.

    Allophones : Allophones are the different realizations of the same phoneme. For example, English /k/ has several allophones like—aspirated /k/, unaspirated /k/, retracted /k/, advanced /k/ etc.

VOWELS

There are three criteria that determine the vowels : (a) Tongue-part ; (b) Tongue-height, and (c) Position of lips.

Tongue Part : The tongue moves in all directions with its front, blade and its hack. Its movements are responsible for three different kinds of vowels : Front, Central and Back.

Tongue-height : The tongue moves towards the palate, takes the parallel positions or moves to down. These tree positions are called High, Mid and Low.

Lip-rounding : The lip moves to close, half-close, half open and open position in the mouth.

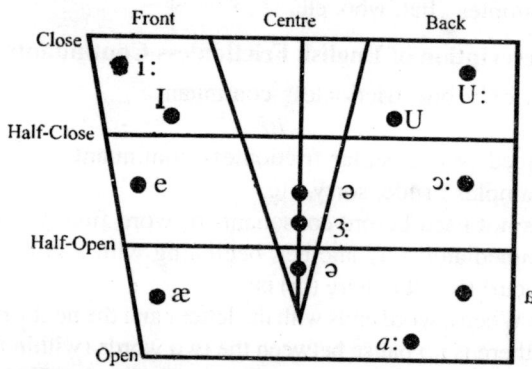

Different tongue positions are shown below :
/i:/—Front close unrounded vowel.
/i/—Centralized front half-close unrounded vowel.
/e/—Front unrounded vowel between half-close and half-open.
/æ/—Front unrounded vowel just below the half position.
/a:/—Back open unrounded vowel
/a/—Back rounded vowel just above the open position.
/ɔ:/—Back rounded vowel between half-open and half-close.
/ʊ/—Centralized back rounded vowel just above half-close.
/U:/—Back close rounded vowel.
/ə/—Central unrounded vowel between open and half-open.
/3:/—Central unrounded vowel between half-close and half-open.
/ə/—Central unrounded short vowel.
(This vowel (ə) only occurs in unaccented syllables.)

Note : Some phoneticians (regarding second front vowel) prefer /I/ ; some prefer /i/.

DIPHTHONGS

There are eight diphthongs in English.
Diphthongs are of three kinds (in respect of the direction of their glides)
(a) **Closing diphthongs gliding to /I/**
English has three closing dipthongs gliding to /I/ :
/ei/, /ai/ and /ɔ i/
/ei/—The glide begins from a point just below the half-close front position and moves in the direction of /i/ (see the figure).
/ai/—The glide begins from slightly behind the front open position and moves towards the RP/i/.

/ɔi/—The glides begins from a point between the back half open and open positions and moves towards the RP/i/.

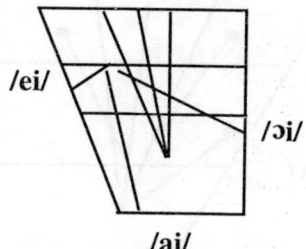

Closing diphthongs gliding to /I/

(b) **Closing diphthongs gliding to /u/—**
English has only two closing diphthongs gliding to /u/:
/au/ and / u/

/au/—The glide begins at a point between hack and front positions and moves to the direction of RP/ʊ/.

/ ʊ/—The glide begins at a central position between half-open and half-close and moves towards RV/ʊ/. (see the following figure)

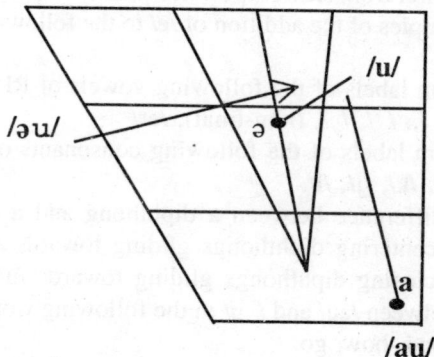

(c) **Centering diphthongs gliding towards / / /i/, /e / and /u/**

/i /—The glide starts (almost) half-close centralized front RP vowel/I/ and moves towards RP vowel/ /.

/e /—The glide starts in the front, just above the half-open position, and moves towards RP vowel / /.

/ʊ /—The glide starts with a tongue position almost that of RP/u/ and moves in the direction of RP vowel / /.

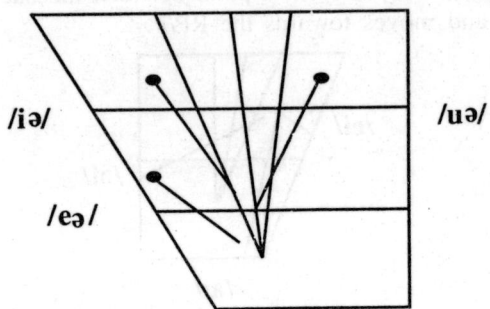

Triphthong : The diphthong +/ / is treated as one vowel phoneme. This vowel phoneme is triphthong.
Examples : player—/pler /.

EXERCISE

1. Describe the diphthongs of the following words :
   Player, layer, fire, iron, slower, power, shower, employer.
2. Give four examples of the addition of /e/ to the following dipthongs :
   /ei/, /ai/, /au/
3. Give three term labels of the following vowels of RP :
   /aI/, au/, /i/, / /,. / /, / /, (non-final), /er/
4. Give three term labels of the following consonants of RP :
   /f/, /v/, /p/, /t/, /k/, /j/, /l/.
5. What is the difference between a diphthong and a triphthong?
6. Describe the centering diphthongs gliding towards / /.
7. Describe the closing diphthongs gliding towards /u/.
8. Distinguish between /au/ and / u/ in the following words : row, load, no, known, loud, bow, go.

Description of Consonants, Vowels & Diphthongs   159

Theory of Distinctive Features

The theory of Distinctive Features was explained by the linguist Roman Jakobson. It deals with the phonetic properties of speech sounds. Phonemes differ from each other in terms of features like **Voice, Place of Articulation, Manner of Articulation** and so on. The vowels are different on the basis of **Lip Rounding, Position of the Tongue, Tongue-part** and so on. This theory proposes a model to describe the sounds with sets of ±. This proposition is binary as the alternatives are only tow (+) or (–) :

Classificatory Features
± consonatal
± vocalic
± syllabic
± obstruent
(Sounds which create a radical obstruction of the airflow vs which do not behave in the same way).
± nasal

Articulatory Features
± high
± low
± back
± round
± coronal
(Sounds articulated with the blade of the tongue raised from the normal position vs those where this is not applicable.)
± lateral

Manner Features
± continuant
± delayed rebase

Acoustic Features
± voice
(Voiced segments are + voice, voiceless segments are –voice.)
± strident
(High-frequency noise vs not high frequency noise).

PHONETIC TRANSCRIPTION

The IPA (International Phonetic Alphabet) can be used to represent in writing the sounds, words, phrases and sentences of all the languages of the world. This representation is known as Phonetic Transcription. 'Phonemic transcription' and 'allophonic transcription' are the two important varieties of phonetic transcription. In phonemic transcription phonemes of the languages are represented whereas in allophonic transcription even the allophonic variations are represented.

Now we shall transcribe (phonemic) some English words at random:

pack	—	/pæk/	life	—	/aif/
feel	—	/fi:l/	shot	—	/ʃat/
kat	—	/kæt/	shoe	—	/fʊ:/
wet	—	/wet/	ship	—	/ʃip/
men	—	/men/	edition	—	/idiʃn/
she	—	/ʃi:/	register	—	/red3istə/
bed	—	/bed/	recollect	—	/rekələkt/
calm	—	/ka:m/	recollection	—	/rek lekʃn/
absolute	—	/æbs ljut/	original	—	/erldzənl/
accident	—	/æksident/	embrace	—	imbreis/
simple	—	/simpl/	decrease	—	/di:kri:s/
silicone	—	/silikeun/	decade	—	dikeid/
sick	—	/sik/	cutting	—	/kʌtiγ/
love	—	/lʌv/	cuckoo	—	/kukʊ/

Now we shall try phonemic transcription of sentences :

The single oblique bar [/] represents the tone group boundary and the double oblique bar [//] represents the end of sentence.

What are you talking about → // wɒt əju to:kiŋə baut //
I am delighted → // aim dilaitid //
Good morning, father → // gud m :niŋfa:ð ə//
I'm a visiting teacher there // aim viztiŋ titʃəðə(r) //
I do teach English → // ai du ti:tʃ iŋgliʃ //
Thanks, my dear, Sir → θæŋks mai di əsə //
She arrived last night → // ʃi raivd la:st nait //
I hate cheap literature → // ai heit tʃi:plitr ətʃ //
I am in trouble → // aim in trʌbl //
Something will turn up → // sʌmθiŋel tə:n p //
Love is too deep → /iʌviz tu: di:p/

EXERCISE

1. What is IPA? What is 'Phonetic Transcription'? Is there any difference between 'phonemic transcription' and 'allophonic transcription'?

2. Write phonemic transcription of the following texts :

(a) He took me into the cabin where his wife and their three-year-old daughter was sitting. The cabin was dark. I could not see anything except the daughter and her mother. I gave them some medicine. "How are they?" he asked. I was little confused. I said, "Not good." I couldn't see his pale face in the darkroom.

(b) The need for learning Spoken English has grown enormously all over the world. English is the "window on the world". Speech is primary. We communicated our feelings / contexts through speech. Speech comes first for us. After that we gradually learn to write. Therefore, Phonetics and Spoken English should be in the prescribed curricula. Students, don't you think so? Let's hope for the best.

(c) I met Mr. Subramanian near the stall. He was (patiently) waiting for me. I was in a hurry because I had to catch a train bound for Pune. He asked me to go through his book on human personality. I asked him, "When are you coming to our University?" He did not reply. I understood his unuttered words. Meanwhile, the train started to move. And I had to rush back to my 'reserved' seat.

(d) A met you at least thousand times. And in most cases I met you in the dead silence of night. You gave me troubles as well as pleasure. You made me feel happy and unhappy. My dreams, you are true and false. You dupe me. You predict 'What is to come.' I love you. I am afraid of you too.

STRUCTURE OF THE SYLLABLE AND PHONEME SEQUENCE

The phonemes are combined to form a relatively higher unit. This unit is known as 'syllable'. A word consists of one or more than one syllable. For Example:

account → e ac-count
/ə-kaunt/
allot → al-lot
/ə-lɒt/

A syllable consists of one or more than one speech sounds. The speech sounds can be vowels or consonants. The vowel element in a syllable is a must. Therefore, the vowel element is known as the nucleus (of a syllable). The consonant occupies the marginal position of a syllable. The consonant that begins a syllable is called releasing consonant. And the consonant that occurs at the end of a syllable is called arresting consonant. We refer to vowel and consonant as v and c respectively.

Examples : (i) girl—/gɜ:l/
c v c
(ii) street—/stri:t/
c c c v c
(iii) ask—/a:sk/
v c c
(iv) subtle—/s –tl/
c v c vʌ

Types of Syllable

1. Only V type :
    Word — V (structure)
    I — /ai/
    a — /ə/

2. Only VC type :
    Word — VC (structure)
    all — /ɔ:l/
    a — /æm/

3. CV type :
    Word — CV (structure)
    See — /si:/
    go — /gəu/

4. CVC Type :
    Word — CVC (structure)
    cry — /krai/
    play — /plei/

Structure of the Syllable and Phoneme Sequence

5. VCC type :

        Word   —   VCC (structure)
        and   —   /ænd/
        apple —   /æpl/

In the same way we get the types :

        cccv   cvcccc
        cccvc   ccvcccc
        cccvcc   ccvcc
        cccvccc   cvcc
        vccc

The maximum possible structures are :

C_{0-3} VC_{0-4} or (CCC) V (CCCC)

Syllabic Consonants

Sometimes a consonant (like /n/, /l/ and /m/) takes the position of the mucleus of a syllable. When a consonant behaves like a vowel is known as syllabic consonant.

Examples

        mutton—/mvtn/
            c v c v

(Here /n/ is a syllabic consonant)

        subtle—/s$_\Lambda$tl/

(Here /l/ is a syllabic consonant)
prism—/prizm/
     ccvcv

(Here /m/ is a syllabic consonant)

Consonant Clusters—Sequence of consonants at the beginning (maximum of three consonants) or at the end (maximum of four consonants) of a syllable occur together. They are called consonant clusters.

For Example,

(i) straw→/str :/
     cccv

Here /str—/is a consonant cluster.

(ii) accident→/æk-si-dent/
     vc-vc-cvcc

Here /-nt/ is a consonant cluster in 'dent'.

(iii) pretest→/pre-test/
     ccv-cvcc

Here /pr-/ and /-st/ are consonant clusters in 'pre' and 'test' respectively.

Phonemic transcription and Syllable Division

circus—/sə:-kes/,
    cv cvc
cigarette—si-g -ret/.
    cv cv cvc
english—/ing-lif/
    vcc-cvc
sudden—/sʌ-dn/
    cv cv
remember—/ri-m m-b/
    cv cvc cv
names—/neimz/
    cvcc

battle—/bæ-tl/
    cv-cv
beauty—/bju:-ti/
    ccv-cv
brilliant—/bri-lient/
    ccv-cv-vcc
spray—/sprei/
    cccv
student—/stju:-dnt/
    ccv-cvc
churches—/tʃə:-tʃiz/
    cv-cvc

WORD ACCENT

Accent in a syllable is said to be associated with relative degree of prominence. Syllable which is prominent are accented. For example:

        prob-lem
        in-di- vi-dual
        mi- grate
        e- co-no-my

Some Rules to be Remembered

(i) The prefix a—and be—are not accented :
a- like, a- bout, be- tween etc.

(ii) The following monosyllabic prefixes are generally accented :
ad—, af—, ag—, al—, an—, ar—, as—, ab— etc.
Examples:
an—nex, ac—cent, ad—dict etc.

(iii) Inflectional suffixes and some derivational suffixes do not affect the general accent:

boxes, wanted, going, happening, beautiful, smartness, thankless, entrance, whitewash, friendship, citizen, boyish.

The derivational suffixes –ance, –ful, –hood, –ness, –ly, –ship, –ter, –zen, –ess, –ish do not generally affect the accent.

(iv) –aire, –ean, –ee, –een, –eer, –oo, –ese, –esque, –ette, –eum—these suffixes are generally accented.

Examples

millio'naire, jaco'bean
exmploy'ee, can'teen, ta'boo,
profi'teer, chi'nese
gro'tesque, ga'zette

(v) Words ending in –ic, –ical, –ically, –ions, –ial and –ially take the accent on the syllable preceding the suffix.

Examples

pa–'the-tic
e'-lec-trical
ma–the–'ma–tically
no–'to–rious
me–'mo–rial
com–'mer–cially
Exceptions—'rhetoric, 'lunatic etc.

(vi) Words ending in –graphy, –logy, –scopy, –metry, –phony are accented on the syllable immediately preceding the ending.

Examples
ge–'o–graphy
bi–'o–graphy
bi–'o–logy
ge–'o–metry
'sym–phony
ra–di–'o–scopy.

(vii) Verbs (disyllabic) ending–ize (–ise) receive the accent on the ending :
ad–'vise
de–'vise
cap–'size
Exception—'realize

(viii) For verbs of three / four syllables (ending –ize or –ise) the accent falls on the third syllable from the ending :
'cri—ti—cize
 3   2   1
Exception–'cha—rac—ter—ize
           4   3   2   1

(ix) For verbs of five /six syllables (ending –ise or –ize), the accent falls on the fourth syllable from the ending :
le–'gi – ti – ma – tize
 4   3   2   1
Exception—
de–a–'gram–ma–tize
        3   2   1

(x) Disyllabic '–ate' ending verbs are accented on the ending itself :
cry–'ate
mi–'grate

(xi) Words ending in –ion take the accent on the penultimate syllable :
ex–a–mi–'na–tion
de–co–'ra–tion

Accent in Compound Words
Compounds are composite words, made up of several words (separate).

In most compound words the primary accent (will be discussed in the later portion of this chapter) falls on the first of the two elements:
'postman
'tea–break
'rain–coat

For compounds with –ever and –self as the second element the primary accent falls on the second element :
what'ever
her'self

Word Accent

For compounds like afternoon, vice-chancellor, good-looking, home-made, hand-made both the elements get the accent. The primary accent falls on the second element and the first element gets the secondary accent (will be discussed below).

Examples
,after-'noon
,vice-'chancellor
,good-'looking
,home-'made
,hand-'made

Primary Accent
"English polysyllabic words contain one or more than one syllables which are more prominent than their neighbours. This salient syllables is achieved not only by stress (energy of articulation) but also by factors relating to pitch, length and inherent quality." (*English Pronouncing Dictionary* by Daniel Jones). Primary accent indicates the 'tonic' syllable.

Secondary Accent
"When more than one syllable in a word stressed, stresses other than the primary must be regarded as secondary." (Daniel Jones *English Pronouncing Dictionary* Page—[xxii]). Secondary stress is marked with placed (,) before the syllable.

Examples of Primary and Secondary accents are shown below with phonemic transcription.
remuneration →/rimju:nerei∫n/
,unac'ceptable→,vneks'eptebl/
con,ventio'nally→kan,ven∫e'næliti/

EXERCISE

1. What is Word Accent?
2. What is the difference between the primary accent and secondary accent?
3. Place the accent (primary) in the following words :
   Electricity, arabic, terrific, random, pronunciation, examination, loving, sweetheart, lifelong, cow-drawn, living, outstanding, heppening, financial, technical, remuneration, accent, linguistics, societal, dictionary, friendship.
4. Divide the following words into syllables : (Use CV structure)
   fanatic, retirement, appointment, painful, live, telecast, cricket, evening, examination, unacceptable, common, wealth, Indian, English, internet, computer, Chinese, commonwealth, systematic, prominent, nothingness, absurdity, modulated, moderation, dictionary.

ACCENT, RHYTHM AND INTONATION

All the words in connected speech do not receive equal degree of prominence. "The choice of the syllable receiving primary accent depends on the meaning the speaker wants to convey." (*'A Text-book of English Phonetics for Indian Students'* by T. Balasubramanian, 1999, New Delhi, P. 145). In normal speech the content words receive accent whereas the grammatical words don't receive accent (normally). The content words are—nouns, adjectives, verbs (other than be), adverbs, etc. The grammatical words are—auxiliary verbs, prepositions, articles, conjunctions and pronouns (personal & relative). But all depends on the speakers' of words in respect of meaning (intended).

Examples
(i) Ram should ˈgo.
(ii) ˈRam should ˌgo
(iii) Ram ˈshould ˌgo
(iv) Meet me in the canˈteen.
(v) Meet ˈme in the canˌteen.
(vi) ˈMeet me in the canˌteen.

Content words are not accented in the following cases:
(i) When these words are repeated in a topic / context:
You ˈwant me to ˈwrite it? I won't *write*.
You ˈwant me to ˈread ˈEmma'? I cann't *read*.
(ii) When the neighbouring words are emphasized:
I ˈdon't *go* there.
I ˈhaven't *got* it.

The grammatical words are accented in the following cases:

(i) When they are emphasized:
But she ˈis going.
I ˈdo feel for you.

(ii) When polysyllabic prepositions occur before pronouns:
I know ˈnothing aˈbout it.

Rhythm—It refers to the recurrence of certain patterns of sound in utterance(s) of a text. It is periodical by nature. English has stress-timed rhythm. Some languages (like Bengali) have syllable-timed rhythm. The strong or prominent syllables (in English) occur at regular intervals of time.

Examples
ˈSunandan has ˈjust reˈturned from ˈDelhi
I ˈasked her to ˈwait at the ˈstation

Strong and Weak Forms: Many English words have two or more pronunciations: (i) strong pronounciation, (ii) weak pronounciation(s).

Examples

Word	Strong form	Weak form	
had	/hæd/	/bed/	
has	/hæz/	/həz/	
have	/hæv/	/həv/	under three
		/v/	different
		/ev/	situations.
would	/wud/	/wed/	under
		/d/	different
		/ed/	situations.
him	/him/	/im/	
at	/aet/	/əf/	

Use of Weak Forms in Sentences—
(i) He will come at ten.→/him ¹k met ten/
   /et/ is the weak from of 'at'.
(ii) He would be happy→/hi:d bi hæpi/
   /d/ is the weak form of 'would'
(iii) I need a pencil→e/aini :d epensil/
   /e/ is the weak form of 'a' (/ei/ is the strong form)

Intonation—Every language has speech melody. Monotone (with same musical note) is not a characteristic of any language in the world. Different pitches and tones together constitute the intonation of a language.

Some determining Factors of Intonation

(i) Tone group—It is a stretch of speech over which one (only) pattern of pitch variations extends. The tone group is indicated by an oblique (/) sign :
  (a) Please go there / if you don't like me.
  (b) I would like to finish this assignment / before Mrs. Sen comes. (ii) Tonic Syllable—Tonic syllable acts as the nucleus of the tone group. It initiates a change in pitch movement.

Examples
I ¹want Dishari to ¹take the ¹car in the 'park.
('Park' is the tonic syllable.)
Intonation plays a great role in speech. It distinguishes different types of sentences. Even the grammatically indentical sentences can mean differently through different use of intonation :
   She goes to Jhargram. (Statement)
   She goes to Jhargram? (Question)
   She goes to Jhargram! (Surprise)

Intonation is important to communicate the intended message properly with proper way. By 'proper way' we mean the manner of production. The same sentence can be put differently (with different intonations):
ˈOpen the ˈwindow. (Command)
ˈOpen the window. (Request)
Intonation does the magic (in the above sentences.)

Use of Tones—Some Useful Patterns

English has three basic intonation patterns:
(a) Falling tone
(b) Rising tone
(c) The Falling-rising tone.
(English has also Rising—falling tone)
Falling tone is of two kinds—(a) Low Fall and (b) High Fall.
In Low Fall the pitch falls from mid to very low (See the following Fig.)

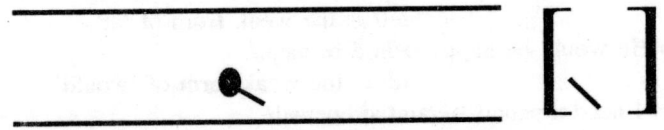

In High Fall the pitch falls from very high to very low (see the following Fig.) :

Falling Tone: The falling tone is used for the following purposes :
   (a) For making simple statements :
        The pen is 'lost.
        'No, You 'did. (expressing strong agreement or disagreement)
   (b) For Wh-Questions :
        Who's your 'father?
        When shall we three go?
   (c) Yes/ No Questions :
        Is he going?
        Cound you go there?
   (d) For exclamations :
        Dear sweetheart!
        What a fine morning!

(e) For commands /Requests :
   Sit down.
   Open the gate.

Rising Tone : Rising tone is used for the following purposes :

(a) For Wh-Questions (for inquiry / concern) :
   What's wrong?
   How is Kaberi now?

(b) For question (not necessarily expecting agreement) :
   You do drink, don't you?
   She studies in Contai College, isn't it?

(c) For making plain statements into questions :
   You like, it?'
   The trains, late?
   It's not in, Jadavpur?

(d) For questions answerable by Yes / No :
   Have you 'been to, CIEFL?
   Was she 'present yesterday?

Like Falling tone, Rising tone too are of two kinds :
   Low Rise and High Rise
Low Rise—The pitch rises from low to mid level.
High Rise—The pitch rises from low to high.

Falling-rising tone : This tone is used for the following purposes :

(a) For incomplete statements :
   If you don't if you don't go,......
   You may go.....

(b) Statements which indicate reservation on the part of the speaker :
   She is faithful. (but the speaker is not sure of it)
   He is good in Mathematics. (but the speaker is doubtful)

Rising falling tone : This tone is used for the following purposes :

(a) For statements showing enthusiastic agreement :
   of course.
   It is fine.

(b) For exclamations (expressing sarcasm/irony) :
   oh, yes. (ironical)
   Well written! (ironical)

EXERCISES

1. What are the conditions for using falling tone?
2. What are the conditions for using rising tone?
3. When do we use falling rising tone?
4. What is intonation? What is a tone group?
5. Divide the following into tone groups. Indicate tone group boundary with oblique bar :
   (i)   I've great regards for him.
   (ii) I like to read Badal Sircar's plays.
   (iii) When shall we meet again?
   (iv) Strange! you are not coming?
   (v)   I went to her hostel in Salt Lake.
   (vi) Of course, she is a noble hostess.
   (vii) I like winter than summer.
   (viii) If you do this.....
   (ix) Please pass the salt to him.
   (x)   Students, sit down.
6. Divide the following paragraph in tone groups:
   (i) I started my teaching career in Santiniketan, a place known for its own culture. The students I came across were really good. They used to obey their teachers. Some of my students became doctors, some became the engineers and some of them took up 'general stream' as their career. Life went on. I grew up in years. Now things have changed. Life around me is different, and the golden days are no more. People say, "Your first job is the best one."
   (ii) "Where are you going?" he asked, I was in a hurry, I could not hear his words. I just passed by giving him a meaningful smile. Next Sunday, I met him again. This time he smiled at me and passed by. I got the fitting response.
   (iii) Life has its own charm. It is beautiful only if we can make it beautiful. People say, "Life is Life." Life is all-inclusive. It is a rosary of joy and sorrow. Life is a journey. And we are but to complete that journey.
   (iv) It is the time for the SAARC literature. The writers from India, Bangladesh, Srilanka, Pakistan are writing in good, acceptable English. This new literature can find its place in University curricula. And the students can feel at home it it. Don't you think so?
   (v) "Where are you going?" I asked him. "I'm going to Goodlands hotel," he replied. I was little confused. "How can

he go to Goodlands?" I asked myself. "He never eats anything in a hotel!" my other half answered. My inquisitiveness ran wild. I started to follow him "He stopped in front of a cinema hall!"

(vi) The notion of the text is semantic rather than grammatical. It means text is seen in the context of its meaning and not in its grammatical arrangement. Even one single sentence can become a text but this kind of text is rare. Texture is the linguistic quality which binds sentences into texts based on various kinds of features such as meaning, cohesion, situation and register.

(vii) Bibhu Padhi has published his poems in distinguished magazines, periodicals and journals throughout the world. He infuses his poems with feelings that question his cultures and his own links with nature.

(viii) Dora comes to say 'good bye'. It is early February and a Jewish festival is taking place. All the children in the neighbourhood are in fancy dress. The men wear their black suits and hats, not some have put on red noses. The women bustle about carrying cakes in boxes.

SPOKEN ENGLISH IN INDIA

Language is used for linguistic communication. We learn to speak first. Then we learn to write. Spoken English serves the practical purpose.

In the linguistically and culturally pluralistic Indian subcontinent English is spoken variously in the different parts of the country. We cannot expect a uniform standard of pronunciation for a foreign language in such a multi-cultural and multi-lingual country. India is a vast and almost an endless country where different cultures co-exist side by side. In India, English occupies the status of Second Language (L 2). Indians learn English after their Mother Tongue (L 1). Therefore, their First Language (L 1) plays a great role in pronunciation, morphological syntactical and stylistic use of English (language). This 'L 1' factor is famous as Mother Tongue Interference or "Mother-Tongue-Pull".

For Example

Bengali, speakers of English use /f/ as bilabial whereas in standard English /f/ is labio-dental.

Malayalee English (M.E.) has a vowel system of 19 vowels (12 Monophthongs and 7 diphthongs).

The term 'Indian English' is all inclusive. Within 'Indian English' there are basic differences. Telugu English, Panjabi English, Bengali English etc. are socio-linguistic realities today. To prescribe the working solution to the problem, General Indian English (GIE) is introduced. It is both a descriptive and prescriptive model. It is free from the gross regional feat of several varieties of 'Indian English'. Some basic characteristics of GIE are discussed below (See the Chart):

(i) GIE has a consonant system consisting of 23 consonants.

(ii) GIE has six diphthongs and eleven pure vowels.

(iii) GIE /i/ and /v/ are closer than RP /I/ and /V/.

(iv) GIE model has $\frac{/t/}{\Pi} \frac{/d/}{\Pi}$ (dental plosive) instead of English fricatives /θ/ and /δ/.

(v) GIE has only /e/ sound whereas RP has /v/, /e/, /3:/

(vi) GIE has many supra-segmental differences (like in accent, intonation, etc.) too.

Assimilation and Elision

Assimlation: Assimilation is a process in which sounds influence each other. Suppose XYZ are three sounds. These sounds constitute a word. Sound X may be replaced by sound under the strong influence of Y. One sound gets influenced by its neighbouring sounds. This very process is known as

Counsonantal Phonemes (23) in GIE

Place	Bilabial		Labio-dental		Dental		Alveolar		Post-alveolar		Retrofled		Palato-alveolar		Palatal		Velar		Glottal	
Manner	Vl	Vd	Vl	Vd	Vl	Vd	Vl	Vd	Vl	Vd	Vl	Vd	Vl	Vd	Vl	Vd	Vl	Vd	Vl	Vd
Plosive	p pin —	p bin —	tʰ thin —	d then —							t tin —	d din —					k kin —	g gun —		
Affricate													tʃ church —	dʒ jam —						
Fricative			f fine —				s sin —	z zip —					ʃ ship —	ʒ pleasure —					h hen —	
Nasal		m man —						n nice —										n king —		
Literal								l love —												
Trill/tap								r read —												
Friction-less continuan				v vine —														well		

assimilation. These assimilatory changes can be both phonemic and allophonic. Assimilation can be progressive assimilation and regressive assimilation :

Progressive assimilation :
pleasure
Here /l/ is voiceless alveolar dental because of the influence of [pʰ] that precedes it.
pleasure : /p/ influences /l/.
(operative influence) P leasure
Regressive assimilation :
Here /l/ is voiced dental lateral due to the strong sounds (θ) that follows /l/.
heal th : (θ) influences /l/.
(operative influence)

Elision: While pronouncing the unaccented sounds quickly some English sounds are elided. This process is known as elision. For examples :

(a) /t/ in elided in last day (/la : s dei/)
(b) /t/ in kept is elided in kept quiet. (/kepkwait/)

Both assimilation and elision are common even in the English speech of native speakers of English. We frequently use these two techniques (knowingly or unknowingly) in Indian English conversations.

EXERCISE

1. What is GIE? Discuss some of its features with examples from 'Indian English.'

BIBLIOGRAPHY

Ashby, P. *Speech Sounds,* London : Routledge. 1995
Balasubramanian, T. *A Textbook of English Phonetics for Indian Students,* New Delhi : Macmillan, 1981.
Bansal, R.K. and Harrison J.B. *Spoken English in India.* Madras : Orient Longman, 1983.
Gimson, A.C. *A Practical Course of English Pronounciation.* London : Edward Arnold, 1975.
Hawkins, P. *Introducing Phonology,* London : Routledge, 1992.
Jones, Daniel. *English Pronouncing Dictionary* (14th edition) New Delhi : Universal Book Stall, 1994.
Laver, Joh. *Principles of Phonetics.* Cambridge: Cambridge University Press, 1994.
Sethi, J. and P.V. Dhamija, *A Course in Phonetics and Spoken English,* New Delhi : Prentice-Hall of India Private Limited, 1998.
Steton, R.H. *Motor Phonetics.* 2nd. ed. Amsterdam: North Holland, 1951.
Tibbitts, E.L. *Practice Material for the English Sounds.* Cambridge: Heffer 1960.

Index

Acceptability	90-91	Contrastive distribution	54
Accent rute	165-166	Craft skills	98
Acoustic Phonetics	137	Coronal	147
Addition of phoneme	17	David, Crystal	03
Adjective inflectional suffix	10	Das, M.	97
		Deep structure	56-62
Affixation	9-12	Deletion	69-85
Allophone	155	Dell Hymes	90
Ambiguity	69-75	Demonstrative	5, 27
American descriptive linguistics	53	Derivational	09, 11-13
		Dependent unit	19-20, 22
Anterior	138	Diachronic	52
Articulatory phonetics		Dialect	95-96
Arete	98	Discourse	90
Article features		Disguise preposition	37
Aspect		Diphthong	156-157
Assimilation	174-175	Distance Education	107-108, 123
Astādhyāni	03	Distinctive features	
Anditory phonetics		Distribution	144
Auxiliary	41	Dodson, C.J	113
Balasubramanian, T.	164	Elision	173
Barthes, R.	97	Embedding	62
Bilingualism	119-120	Empty category principle	86
Bottom up	114	Fallacy	03
Bound morpheme	08	Falling tone	166
Broca's area	01	Falling-risinbg tone	167
Case grammar	86	Formative evaluation	
CD representation		Ferdinand de saussure	03, 52
Classifier	06, 27	Free morpheme	08
Code mixing	92	G B Theory	86
Communicative Competence	90	George Cardone	
		General Indian English (GIE)	174-175
Communicative methodology	114-116	H.E. Palmer	133
Componential Theory	89	IC analysis	18-23
Complementary distribution	54	Idiolect	96
Compounding	14-16	Indian English	91-92
Contracted forms	09, 155	Indianization	92

Interlanguage	101	Pulmonic egressive	137
Intonation	168	Pulmonic ingressive	147
Isogloss	96	Quantifier	05
Joseph Conrad Syndrome	129	Register	96-97
Jacques Derrida	97	Relative clause	
Kernel sentence	58	Rising-tone	167
Langue	52	Roman Jakobson	154
Leonard Bloomfield	03, 53	Rhythm	164
Liquids	145	Sarangi, J.	132
Lopa	03	Scanning	124
Loss of Phoneme	17	Secondary accent	163
Minimal pair	53	Skimming	124
Modal	26	Structural dependence	02
Mohanty, Niranjan	134-137	Stylistics	94-95
Morphology	8-10	Summative evaluation	98
Morphophoninics	16-17	Syllabic Consonant	163
Mother-tongue pull	160	Syllabus designing	118-120
Mutually exclusive	54	Systematic Functional	
Nasal sound	145	Grammar	86
Neuroanatomic structure	143	Top-down	124
Noam Chomsky	01, 93.94, 111	Topicalization	85
Noun Phrase	25-36	Transformational Generative	
Oridinal		Grammar	83
Pānini	03	Triphthong	158
Parole	52	Verb group	46-50
Paradigmatic	52	Voiced Sound	148
Pattern congruity	55	Voiceless sound	148
Pattern Poetry	103	Wernick's area	01-02
Phatic communion	113	X-bar theory	87-88
Phone	53	Yalden, J.	108
Phonology	53	Yes / No Questions	166
Portmanteau morph	08	Zero infinitive	03
Postcolonialism	99-103	Zero morph	08
Psycholinguistics	94-95		

(Reference)